CONTENTS

"There is but one straight course, and that is to seek truth and pursue it steadily."

— George Washington

INTRODUCTION

"A REPUBLIC – IF YOU CAN KEEP IT"

The American Ideal is easy in principle…

". . . WE hold these Truths to be self-evident, that all Men are created equal, that they are endowed by their Creator with certain unalienable Rights, that among these are Life, Liberty, and the Pursuit of Happiness—That to secure these Rights, Governments are instituted among Men, deriving their just Powers from the Consent of the Governed."

… however, although most Americans profess to believe the above in principle, things fall apart in practice. Because of this disconnect, America is marching in ignorance toward the cliff of socialism. We have betrayed our founding principles and are committing slow suicide.

We have become a divided people and spend our time squabbling about things of little consequence on the deck of a sinking ship. Meanwhile, the enemies of freedom blow holes in the ship from without and within.

In one sense, this state of affairs is not so unusual. After all, this has been the lot of humanity for centuries, even for Democracies. Democracies always wind up committing suicide once the general public becomes corrupt enough to believe they can vote themselves benefits from the government, instead of earning them. (Power lusting politicians are of course all too happy to comply).

This leads to the type of political division and conflict that has appeared anywhere humans have had to live in one place with each other for any length of time. The Founders knew human nature. Legend has it that after the Constitutional convention in 1787, when Benjamin Franklin was asked what type of government had been created, he answered, "A Republic—if you can keep it."

However, in another sense, it is surprising and tragic to see this division and this steady slide toward socialism in America. Why? America is the one country in history founded on a specific set of ideas and principles. These principles were designed not to divide, but to unite us as one people—people committed to the proposition that all men are created equal, have unalienable rights, and should therefore be left free. Thanks to the wisdom of our Founders, America was formed as a Constitutional Republic, not a Democracy.

The motto selected as the official seal of the new American government was "E Pluribus Unum," or "out of many, one." This perfectly encapsulated the fact that an extremely diverse group of people were becoming united by the power of an idea, rather than by race, class, ethnicity, geography, conquest or religious creed.

That idea is still best expressed in one word…

LIBERTY

Although the word has been used an abused over the past two centuries, it is still the one word that best encapsulates the concept of the free and independent individual.

> What light is to the eyes – what air is to the lungs – what love is to the heart, liberty is to the soul of man. Without liberty, the brain is a dungeon, where the chained thoughts die with their pinions pressed against the hingeless doors.
> —Robert G. Ingersoll

To America's Founders, securing Liberty for each and every individual was the goal and the end of government. Once Liberty was secured, it was up to free men and women to make something of their lives and provide for themselves through industry and self-reliance. To be an American used to mean that you accepted the fact that your freedom required responsibility. It also meant that you could not claim liberty for yourself unless you fully respected the liberty of others.

The number one problem in this country today is that we have lost any meaningful understanding of what Liberty means in a political context. To me, that's the core issue, because Liberty is an absolute requirement of man's nature. It's non-negotiable. It's also the key that opens the door to the real magic of America. That magic is contained in Jefferson's immortal phrase, "the pursuit of happiness."

The idea that the individual has an unalienable right to pursue his or her own individual happiness is at once the motive force of America and the magnet that continues to draw people from the far-flung corners of the globe.

It is the idea that your individual life has meaning, and that it is your own. It is the idea that no matter what your background, your upbringing, your station in life, you can achieve your dreams and goals as long as you are willing to pursue them and achieve them through your own efforts. It is the idea that your destiny is in your own hands, that it is not determined by fate, nor is it proscribed to you by your parents or your community or your government.

This is what is commonly called the American Dream, and there are as many variations of it as there are Americans. But it is this dream, this idea of individual liberty and self-made destiny that has united millions of people of differing cultures, religions, races, ethnic origins, languages, and beliefs, and enabled them to live together in these United States for two centuries in relative harmony and cooperation.

Historically, that is a unique phenomenon. However, it will not continue if the American people do not have an abiding respect for one another's Liberty and the concept of Individual Rights.

We simply can't afford to lose or give up on the idea of Liberty as the only just and proper organizing principle of this society. This is especially important today as we are at war with those who seek to destroy Liberty anywhere it shines. Tragically, while our brave men and women in the military wage this war abroad, we are swiftly letting Liberty erode at home. We have been drifting in the wrong direction for almost 100 years and we are currently in the midst of an unprecedented lurch toward statism and socialism.

How could this be happening in America? How could we possibly be trying to make watered down versions of socialism and fascism work here in the "land of the free"— especially considering the history of the 20th century?

I believe the answer can be found in two things: (1) the tremendous ignorance of much of the population about the principles of liberty as well as their value; and (2) the fact that both major political parties share fundamental premises that are at odds with the American Ideal of Liberty.

The purpose of this book is to try to bring back to life the principles of Liberty and show the critical importance of upholding Individual Rights consistently and without compromise. It is only the American Ideal of 1776 — LIBERTY — that can unify and get this country moving forward again. Human nature has not changed since 1776, and upholding Liberty as an absolute is still—and will always be—the best path to peace, security, happiness, and prosperity for all.

However, we cannot truly restore freedom in this country with conventional thinking. Once the current scourge of socialism is beaten back, we can't simply go back to a different flavor of the same thing under the banner of the other party.

What we really need is an intellectual revolution that goes far beyond the typical ideas of both liberals and conservatives. In fact, what we need is nothing less than a philosophical revolution that does justice to our Founders and allows us to complete what they started by reclaiming our Liberty and securing it for our posterity—for good this time.

I truly hope we can reignite the flame of Liberty before it's too late. We will not like what comes after America.

CHAPTER 1

THE FOUNDATIONS OF FREEDOM

Man is capable of living in society, governing itself by laws self-imposed, and securing to its members the enjoyment of life, liberty, property, and peace. —

In the spring of 1776, the people residing in the thirteen British colonies of America had a problem on their hands. Since the prior spring, after the first skirmishes between the locals and British troops in Lexington and Concord, things had gotten a bit out of hand.

Through the heroic efforts of Henry Knox in obtaining artillery guns from Fort Ticonderoga and dragging them five hundred miles through the snow to Boston, George Washington had been able to end the British siege of Boston that winter. However, by May of 1776, the most powerful Kingdom on earth was now putting its foot down squarely on the neck of these upstart colonists. Thousands of British troops were on American soil, and most of the major cities were in possession of the British. The mighty British navy was hovering along the coast, waiting for any opportunity to go in to burn and destroy defenseless towns and cities.

The colonies were weak, unorganized, quarreling amongst themselves, and without any wealth or arms to speak of. Over the past year, there had been horrific bloodshed at Lexington and on Bunker Hill. The majority of the people wanted to reconcile with the "mother country." They were afraid and most thought that challenging the most powerful nation on earth was foolhardy and victory was impossible. As John Adams wrote, "We were about one third Tories, and one third timid, and one third true blue."

So what did the colonies decide to do? They decided to declare their Independence.

On June 18th, after weeks of debate in Philadelphia, the American Continental Congress appointed a committee to draft a Declaration of Independence from Great Britain. This was effectively a mouse declaring war on a lion and all of the delegates knew it. A vigorous debate ensued. However, on July 2nd, the decision to go forward was made after Cesar Rodney rode his horse 80 miles to arrive in Philadelphia and dramatically cast the deciding vote.

On July 4, 1776, the Declaration was formally adopted by the colonies.

All of the men who were to sign it knew they were risking a death sentence but pledged "their lives, their fortunes, and their sacred honor." It was officially signed on August 2nd, after which, Benjamin Franklin remarked, "Well Gentleman, we must now hang together, or we shall most assuredly hang separately."

The purpose of the Declaration was two-fold. First, it served as a formal document to explain to the world what they were doing and why. They knew they would need the aid of other countries in the effort and wanted to provide a dignified and formal rationale for their actions. And secondly, they wanted to provide a classic statement to the future citizens of America, explaining what their country stood for, so that their children and their children's children could study it and learn it by heart.

On July 8, 1776, "The Unanimous Declaration of the Thirteen United States," was read publicly in the State House yard in Philadelphia and the Liberty bell was rung. In it, was this famous paragraph…

> WE hold these Truths to be self-evident, that all Men are created equal, that they are endowed by their Creator with certain unalienable Rights, that among these are Life, Liberty and the Pursuit of Happiness—That to secure these Rights, Governments are instituted among Men, deriving their just Powers from the Consent of the Governed, that whenever any Form of Government becomes destructive of these Ends, it is the Right of the People to alter or to abolish it, and to institute new Government, laying its Foundation on such Principles, and organizing its Powers in such Form, as to them shall seem most likely to effect their Safety and Happiness.

They signed that declaration, even though they knew it would produce a long, horrible, and bloody war. Most of the signers looked to the future and saw gloom, deprivation, hardships, and death.

So why did they do it? Because, they also saw something else. They saw the rays of FREEDOM.

As John Adams wrote to his wife Abigail after the signing…

> You will think me transported with enthusiasm, but I am not. I am well aware of the toil, and blood, and treasure that it will cost us to maintain the Declaration, and support and defend these States. Yet, through all the gloom, I can see the rays of ravishing light and glory. I can see that the end is more than worth all the means, and that posterity will triumph in that day's transaction.

America Stands For Freedom

America is unique among nations. It is the only country in history founded on an idea, rather than on geography, ethnicity, race, conquest, or other accidents. It was founded on a principle—that principle is the sovereignty of the individual. It is the principle that all men are by nature equally free and independent.

I do not think it's overstating the case to say that the founding philosophy of America represented a basic set of principles and ideas that reflected the most thorough and thoughtful consideration and discussion on how best to organize societies since the beginning of time. This was largely due to the caliber of men that founded this country.

The Founding Fathers were all incredibly well-read in political philosophy, especially Jefferson, Adams, Madison and Franklin. In the Declaration, Jefferson was able to concisely, but powerfully, summarize the culmination of several generations of political thought about Liberty and the relationship between individuals and governments. There was a true spirit of Liberty at the time that does not exist today.

Unlike the politicians of today, the men we call America's Founding Fathers were true intellectuals and statesmen. They were men of the Enlightenment, thoroughly trained in the classical tradition, with an integrated understanding of history, philosophy, politics, and law from the time of the Greeks up to their own time.

In the words of American Philosopher Ayn Rand…

> The Founding Fathers were neither passive, death-worshiping mystics nor mindless, power-seeking looters; as a political group, they were a phenomenon unprecedented in history; they were thinkers who were also men of action. They had rejected the soul-body dichotomy, with its two corollaries; the impotence of man's mind and the damnation of this earth; they had rejected the doctrine of suffering as man's metaphysical fate, they proclaimed man's right to the pursuit of happiness and were determined to establish on earth the conditions required for man's proper existence, by the "unaided" power of the intellect.

In their fundamental belief that the purpose of government was solely to guarantee life, liberty, property, and the pursuit of happiness, and in their founding documents, the Declaration of Independence, the Constitution, and the Bill of Rights, they left us a compass and a map.

To the extent that we have followed that compass and map, we have seen steadily increasing wealth and higher standards of living. We have also seen increasing access to it by a constantly growing number of Americans.

Following that compass and map has fulfilled the promise of liberty and "the good life" for more people around the world than any other society on earth. Following that compass and map allowed America to stay on course through rapid changes and countless crises both at home and abroad. For the most part, it allowed us to avoid falling into the totalitarian traps that were all the rage in Europe in the 20th century.

America Is the Country of the Enlightenment

The American Revolution, or more accurately, The War For Independence, was not just about gaining Independence from King George (a very mild tyrant by today's standards). It was the culmination of a 6000 year struggle for the rights of man—for the right of individuals to be free from a controlling Authority.

The key to understanding the success of America is that it was founded at the apex of the Enlightenment. It was a time when the authority of both church and state were being rejected.

America was born in the Age Of Reason, an age where men were sweeping aside the errors of the past, declaring that the universe was intelligible and happiness on earth was possible—as long as men were left free to apply their reasoning minds to the problems they confronted.

This was a profound shift. Throughout human history, men had always been under the control of either barbarians using the club of force, or mystics using the club of "divine knowledge." Political Liberty was something that had never truly existed before.

Even in pre-Industrial England, where the Magna Carta had been written in the 13th century, representing the first formal attempts since Ancient Greece to establish political Liberty, it was still a Liberty granted by permission of the King—it was not acknowledged that men were free by their very nature and therefore possess inherent and inalienable rights. John Adams' son, John Quincy Adams, explained it this way in an address on the fourth of July, 1821...

> The people of Great Britain, through long ages of civil war, extorted from their rulers, not acknowledgements, but grants, of right. With this concession they had been content to stop. They received their freedom as a donation from their Sovereign; they appealed for their privileges to a signed manual and a seal; they held title to their liberty, like their title to their lands, from the bounty of a man; and in their moral and political chronology, the great charter of Runnymead (the Magna Carta), was the beginning of the world. Instead of solving civil society into its first elements in search of their rights, they looked only to conquest as the origin of their liberties, and claimed their rights but as donations from their Kings. This faltering assertion of freedom is not chargeable indeed upon the whole nation. There were spirits capable of tracing civil government to its foundation in the moral and physical nature of man; but conquest and servitude were so mingled up in every part of the social existence of the nation, that these had become vitally necessary to them.

As Adams so clearly puts it, the profound shift made by the original Americans, was their rejection of the idea that one needed to hold title to their

Liberty from "the bounty of a man." They claimed it as an axiomatic part of man's nature and all possessed Liberty because all men were equal.

The word unalienable used by Jefferson in the Declaration is a very important adjective. It means "inherent," "inviolate," and "absolute." It also means "incapable of being surrendered or transferred." In other words, it means a right that cannot be taken away by another because it was not granted by another in the first place. As John Adams said, these rights have their "foundation in the moral and physical nature of man." Notice also that the Declaration says to "secure" these rights governments are instituted among men. They did not believe that governments "create" or "grant" these rights.

I would submit to you that almost the entire world (including a great many people in America), still think today that their rights are not unalienable, but are "donations from their Kings."

To this day, even our enlightened European friends have never fully grasped the concept that an individual lives by right, and not by permission. This is because autocracy is all they have ever known—that has been their frame of reference for centuries. Despite their many wonderful cultural contributions to mankind, their modern political philosophies have been decidedly statist. As a result, Europeans have been conditioned to roll over and submit to the chains of their Nanny states without a whimper. Sadly, many Americans are doing the same thing.

Needless to say, most in the Middle East and Asia don't even have the slightest understanding of this concept of inalienable rights. They too have been under the iron heel of their rulers for centuries.

That's why it is so important to understand the truly revolutionary nature of the American Founding. For the first time in history, a group of men who had political power finally acknowledged that men are free by their very nature; and therefore, no force on heaven or earth could change the fact that a man's life is his own and he should be left free to pursue his own happiness. The only condition placed on that freedom was that he must respect the equal right of others to do the same.

Starting with that history-shattering foundation, the Founders then devised a Government, an "empire of laws and not of men," in the words of John Adams, and turned the world upside down by making that Government the servant of the citizens, instead of the other way around.

The Constitution & Individual Rights

Asserting a theory of "rights" is one thing. Establishing and protecting them via a political system is quite another. The next great achievement of the Founders was the United States Constitution.

The Constitution and the Bill of Rights were intended to limit Government to its proper function in a free society—that of a "policeman" that protects individuals from force and fraud and acts as a "referee" in settling civil and contract disputes when they arise. Unlike the English system that John Adams spoke of, they did not seek to gain their rights from the Government or any Ruler—they claimed them as axiomatic. They knew very well that, because it was granted a monopoly on the use of force, it was government itself that was the greatest threat to freedom.

The Bill of Rights should really be called "The Bill of Constraints on Government"—because they are really prohibitions placed on the Government. The Framers of the Constitution knew that men were free and therefore their rights were already a given. They knew that rights did not derive from the permission of their rulers because they did not have rulers. They were to rule themselves through "self-government."

As we've been discussing, the organizing principle of America is the concept of Liberty, which means the sovereignty of the individual, the freedom of the individual to pursue his own personal values free from government coercion. The Constitution was designed to protect that principle.

John Locke and other Enlightenment thinkers demonstrated that individuals do not exist to serve governments, but rather, governments exist to protect individuals. The individual, said Locke, has an inalienable right to life, liberty, and the pursuit of his own happiness.

The Founding Fathers fully agreed with that premise. The function of government in their view was solely to secure and protect individual rights. As Jefferson wrote in the Declaration, "governments are instituted among men to secure these rights."

Or as the 19th Century French Philosopher and Economist Fredric Bastiat put it, "Life, Liberty, and Property do not exist because men have made laws. On the contrary, it was because life, liberty, and property existed beforehand that caused men to make laws in the first place."

It's important to note that the concept of rights is both absolute and universal, i.e., held by all men simultaneously. There is no such thing as a "right" that violates the rights of another. Legitimate rights impose no obligation or duty on others. This is why there is no such thing as a "right to health care" for example. If I have a "right" to health care, that means you have to provide me with health care at your expense, which is a violation of your rights. Rights simply give us the freedom to think and then act on that thinking in our own rational self-interest.

To put it another way: legitimate rights are rights to action, not to property, benefits or rewards from other people.

As Samuel Adams put it, "Among the natural rights of the Colonists are these: First, a right to life; Secondly, to liberty; Thirdly, to property; together with the right to support and defend them in the best manner they can. These are evident branches of, rather than deductions from, the duty of self-preservation, commonly called the first law of nature."

Mr. Adams points out that there is only one fundamental right: a man's right to his own life. All other rights, such as freedom of speech, freedom of action, freedom of worship, freedom to trade, freedom of association, property rights, etc., are derivatives of that one basic right—the right to self-preservation.

As was his habit, Samuel Adams put it very forcefully and succinctly when he said, "The natural liberty of man is to be free from any superior power on Earth, and not to be under the will or legislative authority of man, but only to have the law of nature for his rule."

This is the key issue that we need to be aware of today – the proper role and sphere of government in a free society. To the Founders, it was extremely clear as you can see from just the few quotes above.

However, we have lost that clarity today and most Americans have a very fuzzy and contradictory view of what the role of government in America really should be. In addition, too many Americans are entirely ignorant of the Constitution and its real purpose. As George Mason University Economics Professor, Walter E. Williams puts it…

In addition to an abhorrence of democracy, and the recognition that government posed the gravest threat to liberty, our founders harbored a deep distrust and suspicion of Congress. This suspicion and distrust is exemplified by the phraseology used throughout the Constitution, particularly our Bill of Rights, containing phrases such as Congress shall not: abridge, infringe, deny, disparage or violate. Today's Americans think Congress has the constitutional authority to do anything upon which they can get a majority vote. We think whether a particular measure is a good idea or bad idea should determine passage as opposed to whether that measure lies within the enumerated powers granted Congress by the Constitution. Unfortunately, for the future of our nation, Congress has successfully exploited American constitutional ignorance or contempt.

Before we can truly understand and appreciate what the role and limitations on government should be (and why), we have to understand the nature of government itself.

Here are two key points:

1. Government is force. Government is not a "service." It's not caretaker, it's not a nanny. A self-governing people delegate their natural right of self-defense to the government in order to have an orderly society based on objectively defined laws that prevent the initiation of force. We give the government a monopoly on the retaliatory use of force in order to preserve rights. The concept of a government limited to that purpose was designed to prevent two things: anarchy on the one hand and tyranny on the other.

2. Government is not a productive enterprise. It creates and produces nothing of its own. Every dime that it has (or used to have) was taken from those that did produce it (taxpayers). There is no "government tooth fairy" that waves a magic wand and creates money. The only way government can provide a benefit for one group is by taking money from another group by force.

"Government is not reason; it is not eloquence; it is force," said George Washington. "Like fire, it is a dangerous servant and a fearful master." Washington knew the true nature of government better than anyone. He was so well respected after the Revolution, most of the people wanted him elected King and he could have served for life. He declined and voluntarily limited his term in order to set a precedent for those who would follow him.

The Founders understood that government poses the gravest danger to society because it holds a monopoly on the use of force. It cannot be emphasized enough that the original purpose of government in America was simply to protect men's rights: to protect them from physical violence and coercion. The job of providing for the needs of society was left to the free men and women of America.

Getting to that point was the culmination of centuries of struggle. As soon as government strays from that purpose, it turns from a protector of rights into a violator of rights. In other words, the government then becomes criminal by engaging in "legalized plunder." America became the most powerful and prosperous country in history because it was designed by the Founding Fathers to be a country that would finally free mankind from the yoke of the state. The political framework was designed to cage the government; to limit the government to one task: the protection of individual rights.

> Rightful liberty is unobstructed action according to our will within limits drawn around us by the equal rights of others. I do not add 'within the limits of the law' because law is often but the tyrant's will, and always so when it violates the rights of the individual.

Jefferson also said, "The legitimate functions of government extend only to those acts which are injurious to others." That's plain enough, isn't it? Or consider this from John Adams:

> The moment the idea is admitted into society that property is not as sacred as the laws of God, and that there is not a force of law and public justice to protect it, anarchy and tyranny commence. If `Thou shalt not covet' and `Thou shalt not steal' were not commandments of Heaven, they must be made inviolable precepts in every society before it can be civilized or made free. —John Adams

As Adams points out, without secure property rights no other rights are possible. Why? Because without the right to keep the product of your own labor you have no means to sustain your life.

We either have a right to the fruits of our own labor or we don't. If men in the government can take "some" of our money without our consent then, in principle, what is to stop them from taking all of it? We all have a limited amount of time on this earth. The time we spend working in order to obtain the money and material goods we need to live is time we can never get back. It is time away from our families, friends and other pursuits. By allowing government to tax us beyond what is proper, they are not only taking our money, they are taking pieces of our life.

Our Founders knew the critical importance of property rights as the foundation of a prosperous society. A government that is limited for liberty protects the property of each and every individual equally and impartially.

The Results of the American Experiment

And what was the result of this unique "experiment" in individual Liberty and this heretofore unheard of thing, "limited" government? The result was unparalleled human progress.

When men were finally freed from the chains of statist oppression, it unleashed a torrent of human intelligence and energy, the likes of which the world has never seen before or since. In roughly one century, the Americans, along with the English, and a few countries in Western Europe, advanced mankind to a far greater degree than had been done in all the centuries prior.

Let's take a look at that in the next chapter…

CHAPTER 2
THE FRUITS OF FREEDOM

From the wheel to the skyscraper, everything we are and everything we have comes from a single attribute of man – the function of his reasoning mind. – Ayn Rand

The founding of the United States meant that the rediscovery of Reason and Science that accelerated during the Enlightenment period was now combined with true political freedom for the first time in history. The results were remarkable.

Think about this…

The first Westerners arrived on this shore only 500 years ago. When they got here they found a huge uncharted continent and faced a barren and hostile wilderness. Whereas the Old World had a pretty advanced civilization at the time, the "New World" did not. It was still in a "pristine" state of nature—which means that it was a wilderness hostile to man, an enemy of human life.

If humans were to survive and thrive here, their task was to first fight off and attack that wilderness, and then use their minds to shape that wilderness in ways that served their needs and enabled their survival and progress. In other words, their task was to build a civilization.

And did they ever.

Even before the Revolution, the colonies were relatively prosperous. The colonists had a high degree of freedom. They were industrious, hard working, and they had a robust economy. However, the War changed all of that and put everything they had worked for in jeopardy. That's one of the reasons that only about one-third of the people supported the War for Independence to begin with.

With the war behind them, and their liberty secured by a written Constitution, the Americans were free to work, invent, and create as never before. They threw themselves full-force into the Industrial Revolution already begun in England and Europe. The progress has been nothing short of astounding.

Americans turned that wilderness into an advanced, modern civilization with prosperous cities and towns throughout every corner of the continent. They defeated darkness through the invention of electricity; they conquered space through steamships, railroads, mass-produced automobiles, airplanes, and rocket ships; they conquered disease through vaccinations and medical treatments; they conquered time through the telegraph, telephones, radio, television, and now the Internet. They defeated hunger through the mass production and distribution of foods of all kinds. They even conquered drudgery through refrigerators, washing machines, dishwashers, and dozens of other labor saving appliances.

In the relatively short period between the Civil War and World War I — a period we should call the "Inventive Age" instead of the Gilded Age — America became an economic juggernaut, as well as the symbol of freedom and prosperity around the world. During those decades, real GDP more than doubled, rising at better than 6% per year, and life expectancy rose by almost 50%. Due to innovations in machinery and production, working hours were shortened as well.

All of this created time for leisure and contemplation, and the dynamic American society developed an infinite variety of sports and entertainment, as well as intellectual and artistic pursuits, to enjoy during that leisure time.

What's more, the entire society benefited from these inventions and economic growth. Class distinctions were obliterated and stories of Americans going from "rags to riches" became too numerous to recount. There was no income tax at the time and very little government regulation, so entrepreneurs flourished. Entrepreneurs and investors could reinvest 100% of their profits back into growing their businesses, which is one of the main reasons for the fast growth, innovation and success of people like Henry Ford.

All of this innovation and expansion created new industries, new employment opportunities, and lower prices for goods. That is the upward spiral of prosperity that true capitalism creates.

A New World Within Three Generations

Upon receiving the reports from Lewis and Clark after their expedition, and realizing how vast the uncharted continent was,
estimated it would take one thousand years for Americans to explore and settle the entire continent. Amazingly, it took less than one hundred years. This rapid expansion and the incredible achievements of the 19th century were not the gifts of gods or kings. They were the inevitable result once man was free to use his mind to its fullest extent.

Now, needless to say, things were not always this way. In fact, for the prior 6000 years it was the lot of most people in all parts of the world to live what Thomas Hobbes described as "miserable, brutish and short" lives.

The strong enslaved the weak. The masses were sick or hungry most of the time (or both). When night fell they were in darkness. The work they had to do was back-breaking and tedious. Traveling was long, arduous and full of risks. There was not much time for thinking or intellectual pursuits. There was not much time for sports or entertainment. Children died before they became adults. The average lifespan was a fraction of what it is today. Widespread poverty was the order of the day.

It's hard for us in the West today to imagine the severity of life in the times prior to our modern era, so let's look at a few concrete examples…

In France, in the 17th century, 25–50% of the population was considered under the poverty line. And what was the standard of the poverty line in those days? It was defined as the ability to afford your daily minimum bread requirement.

In England, under the serfdom of the Middle Ages, the peasant was tied to the land, owed military service to his Feudal Lord, and that Feudal Lord (i.e., the local government) was his judge, jury and executioner all rolled into one. He combined the powers of police, judge and lawmaker into one authority. This left a legacy that continued for hundreds of years. In the middle of the 18th century in London, the numbers of deaths exceeded the numbers of births—by an order of 3 to 1.

Or consider the conditions in Ireland in the 18th and 19th centuries. Long after industrialization had improved England, the economy in Ireland was still based on tenant farming and plagued with the problem of absentee landlords and the repressive policies of the English government.

The tragic famines of Ireland have been well documented, but how bad was it really? "The dire poverty of the 19th century Irish resulted in an average life expectancy of 19 years—compared to 36 years for contemporary American slaves—and the fact that slaves in the United States typically lived in houses a little larger than the unventilated huts of the Irish and slept on mattresses, while the Irish slept in piles of straw."

Today, the vast majority of Americans live like kings compared to most people in pre-Industrial times.

In her 1940 book, *The Discovery Of Freedom*, Rose Wilder Lane (daughter of Laura Ingalls Wilder, author of *The Little House on The Prairie*), asks the following:

> For sixty known centuries, multitudes of men have lived on this earth. Their situation has

> been the everlasting human situation. Their desire to live has been as strong as ours. Their energy has always been enough to make the earth at least habitable for human beings. Their intelligence has been great.
>
> Yet for six thousand years, most men have been hungry. Famines have always killed multitudes, and still do over most of this earth. Ninety-five years ago, the Irish were starving to death; no one was surprised. Europeans have never expected to get from this earth enough food to keep them all alive.
>
> Why did men die of hunger for six thousand years?
>
> Why did they walk and carry goods and other men on their backs, for six thousand years, and suddenly, in one century, only on a sixth of this earth's surface, they make steamships, railroads, motors, airplanes, and now are flying around the earth in its utmost heights of air? Why did families live six thousand years in floorless hovels, without windows or chimneys, then in eighty years and only in these Unites States, they are taking floors, chimneys, glass windows for granted, and regarding electric lights, porcelain toilets, and window screens as minimum necessities.

So why the difference? What explains this? How did people within three generations create a completely new world? Wilder's conclusion was that it was due to the anti-authoritarian nature of the Founding, which removed the state as a barrier to the release of human intelligence and energy. This is largely correct but it goes a little deeper than that—what underlying factors led to this profound change?

The Four Pillars Of America

The success of America was no accident. It was not just by chance that in roughly one hundred years civilization advanced more than in the prior six-thousand years combined. In addition to the fact that Liberty was protected by the political system, there are several other factors that came together and sparked this period of unparalleled advancement.

I would suggest the success of America in its first 125 years was built on four strong pillars as follows:

1. Reason.
2. Liberty.
3. Capitalism.
4. Productive Achievement.

Let's take a look at these four pillars in the context of the original American system.

Reason. A commitment to reason and science (as opposed to faith and obedience to dogma) freed men's minds to think and pursue knowledge—knowledge that could be applied to improving their lives through business, trade, science, technology, and the arts.

Despite what most conservatives say, America was decidedly not founded on faith or religion. Had we been, we would be in the same shape most Muslim countries are today. The reason for our success is not that we are a Christian nation that has been "blessed" by a god. If you study the period closely, you will find that the founding of the American political system was clearly secular in nature, with a strict separation of Church and State. That was by the specific intent of the Founders and for very good reasons. We will discuss this more in later chapters, but make no mistake about it—the United States of America was founded on the rock of reason, not the quicksand of religious faith.

As Jefferson said, "That form which we have substituted, restores the free right to the unbounded exercise of reason and freedom of opinion. All eyes are opened, or opening, to the rights of man."

Liberty. The political principle of Liberty is based on a philosophy of individualism, which means that each man has a right to his own life and property, a right to pursue his own happiness, and a right to keep the fruits of his own labor. Individualism means people strive for self-reliance and take responsibility for themselves, as opposed to being a criminal or relying on the King or the State to take care of you. As a political term, Liberty simply means the freedom to think and act without interference or coercion by the State.

The principle of Liberty is indivisible; meaning, it pertains to all human realms—intellectual, socio-political, and economic. You cannot truly have Liberty in any one area without having it in all three areas. Economic freedom requires political freedom. Political freedom requires intellectual freedom. Intellectual freedom requires a commitment to Reason.

Capitalism. The socio-economic system of capitalism requires men to deal with one other as traders, exchanging value for value, and improving prosperity for everyone willing to work and contribute to productive enterprise. Due to the profit motive, it also encourages investment in the most productive products and inventions and industries.

Capitalism is based on voluntary and mutual exchange instead of coercion and force. Capitalism is simply "what happens," once the government is limited to its proper role as a protector of Liberty and nothing more. When Reason and creative intelligence are valued, and Liberty is fully protected by the State, people realize they won't be able to get what they want by clubbing one another over the head and taking it. So in order to get what you want in a society with a division of labor, you must develop skills and somehow provide value to others. That is Capitalism in a nutshell.

Respect For Achievement. The end result of a Capitalist system is productive achievement. Once freedom of action is insured and the State is not tying men down and controlling them, phenomenal human progress and achievements result. This respect for achievement and self-improvement has been prevalent since the beginnings of America. It can be seen as early as Benjamin Franklin's "Poor Richard" and his maxims for success and achievement, through Napoleon Hill's "Think and Grow Rich" and the modern self-improvement industry.

Fundamentally, the system of capitalism, which is based on the recognition of individual rights and upholds the concept of Liberty, is the system of the free mind. It allows men to think freely, to use their minds to their fullest extent, and then pursue their dreams, visions and goals full tilt and without limit. This is an inherently *good* thing, because in a truly free country, men can only achieve great wealth by earning it—and you can only earn it by providing enormous values to your fellow men on a wide scale.

Contrary to Marxist class warfare nonsense and the mistaken "dog eat dog" view of capitalism, its essence is the creation of value and its method is based on cooperation among men. That is how inventions and innovations happen. That is how values and benefits to mankind are produced. This respect for success and achievement was once a hallmark of American society and culture, but it is tragically on the wane.

These are some of the main themes we'll explore in the following chapters.

If you think about the above four pillars, they may seem obvious, self-evident even. You probably recognize immediately that those are indeed the four ingredients required for advancement, prosperity, and peace.

So why is that everywhere we turn they are under heavy assault?

CHAPTER 3

THE ANTI-AMERICAN REVOLUTION

Fascism is for Liberty. It is for the only kind of Liberty that is serious—the Liberty of the State. — Benito Mussolini

While America and the West were in the period of the greatest achievement, innovation and economic expansion the world had ever seen, a counter-revolution was brewing outside of America.

Those who clung to the ancient and primitive belief that man must be controlled by an Authority were not going to disappear without a fight. While the American Revolution championed Liberty and said that your own happiness was the moral purpose of your life, the anti-American Revolution championed statism and said that sacrificing yourself for the good of others or "society" should be your moral goal.

Statism is the idea that the individual is subordinate to the state or society. To take the dictionary definition, it is "support of or belief in the sovereignty of a state, usually a republic." This is the opposite of the American ideal. Statism is always cloaked in language that emphasizes "the common good" along with a call for the individual to sacrifice for the "community." Well, until America, the world had been there and done it that way for thousands of years—it's called collectivism and it is always enforced by tyranny.

The reaction against individualism has taken many forms in the last two hundred years: Socialism, Communism, Fascism, Nazism, Radical Islam and Welfare Statism, and they all share two things in common:

1. They are all fundamentally opposed to America's founding principles.
2. They are all modern manifestations of the most primitive way to organize society: collectivism.

Contrary to popular belief, it is the modern liberals and "progressives" that are the true reactionaries, the real "troglodytes" and "luddites" (terms liberals love to brand conservatives with), not American Conservatives. True American Conservatives (as opposed to religious conservatives) stand for the most progressive and revolutionary idea in history—the freedom of the individual.

To be clear, I use the term American Conservative above to describe someone who upholds our founding ideals of life, liberty and the pursuit of happiness. The trouble in general with the terms "liberal" and "conservative" is that they are relative terms and thus create a lot of confusion. A conservative used to be someone who wanted to "conserve" the ideals of our founding.

However, since the religious right took over the conservative movement in the 1980s, that is no longer the case. Today's conservatives are more interested in conserving much older ideas, those of Christianity. (We'll discuss this in more detail in Chapter 8). Likewise, a "liberal" used to be someone who wanted to "liberate" man from the rule of the Church and the State. In classical terminology, liberals were for economic as well as intellectual freedom. Today they are for neither. They are committed statists.

This reaction against the American Revolution has wrought profound changes to America in the past century. The compass and map left by the Founders has been lost (or thrown overboard to more exact) and this country is way off course.

The idea that liberty is the proper organizing principle of our society has been replaced with the idea of "social justice." American individualism has been replaced by collectivism. Collectivism means the supremacy of the group and leads to Statism in politics. Socialism is its main variant in modern times.

Various socialist-inspired doctrines have helped create an America that is fundamentally different from the vision of the Founders in ideas of rights, property, family, education, economics, justice, defense, and all types of human relationships.

The goal of the Founders was to have as little government as possible while still maintaining order and peace. "That government governs best which governs least," said Thomas Paine. That view was shared widely by all of the founders and expressed by them over and over.

Do you think that's the view of our politicians today? Not even remotely. And the trouble is, both major political parties today are on the wrong side of our founding principles. Both of them have sold us out in order to expand their power.

The Democrats have gone completely off the deep end and don't care the slightest about Liberty. They apparently no longer even know the meaning of the word.

The Republicans talk a good game about limited government and free markets, but their actions contradict their words. They don't walk their talk.

However, before we discuss the major parties specifically, let me suggest to you that the choice is not really Republican vs. Democrat, liberal vs. conservative, or left vs. right, but rather, a choice of freedom or socialism.

We can either go back up to toward the ideal of freedom, with its consequences of equality, prosperity, peace, and happiness… or we can continue on our downward spiral toward the pit of socialism, with its consequences of stagnation, poverty, group warfare, violence, and despair.

The Individual or the State

When it comes to the best ways of organizing society, new ideas are exceedingly rare.

Since about the middle of the 18th century, when the disastrous faith-based rule of religion (the Dark Ages) had been finally broken in the Western world, there have been two, and only two, schools of political thought.

One school had its roots in Aristotle, was developed primarily by Anglo-Scottish thinkers, and found its ultimate expression in the founding of the United States of America. As we've discussed, this school of thought held that a man had "unalienable" rights to life, liberty, property, and the pursuit of his own happiness.

The result of following this school of thought was the rocket explosion of success that was America in her youth, creating wealth and general prosperity on a scale unprecedented in human history.

In little more than one hundred years, the United States went from being an agrarian society of small farmers to becoming the world's leading industrial power. It should be obvious to anyone that the reason for that unprecedented success was the high degree of political and economic freedom enjoyed by Americans of that time.

If we had continued on the path of true political and economic freedom, the United States would be even further ahead of the rest of the world than we are today, and Americans would enjoy a level of prosperity, health, technology, and employment opportunities perhaps several orders of magnitude greater than we have now.

But unfortunately, there was another school of thought…

The other school had its roots in Plato, was developed primarily by various German and French thinkers, and was given its ultimate expression by a man named Karl Marx and others who followed him. This school of thought holds that, through "social engineering" and "central planning," man can construct a better and more just society, or even a "perfect world."

It requires certain people who know what "the perfect world" consists of, of course, and they are the leaders. The ignorant masses must follow the decrees of the leaders, in their own best interest of course. A long line of French and German thinkers such as Rousseau, Kant and Hegel, seem to have had a penchant for creating collectivist ideologies that claim to answer all the questions of life, and they believed that if the masses would just follow them, it would lead to "utopia," or "universal human emancipation," to use a phrase of Marx.

Well, we've seen their utopias.

Following this school of thought has most famously resulted in the horrors of National Socialism in Germany and the United Soviet Socialist Republics. The death toll from just those two "experiments" with socialist utopias exceeds 150 million (the Communists killed far more than the Nazis). This is not to mention the millions killed in China, North Vietnam, North Korea, Cuba, scores of African and South American countries, and that recently defunct quasi-socialist utopia, Iraq.

In America, it has given us the modern welfare state and turned America from a country with a shared identity, once united in its commitment to liberty, achievement, and justice for all, into a society that is increasingly balkanized into various groups with allegedly conflicting interests, each fighting for the favors of the government kings, czars and commissars.

As we discussed, in the socialist philosophy, the individual exists only to serve the needs of society. This always comes under the banner of "fairness" or "social justice" and of "good intentions."

Sorry, but any ideology that has delivered misery everywhere it's been tried and been responsible for 150 million deaths can no longer claim "love of humanity" or "concern for the people" as its motive:

As the late historian Balint Vazsonyi notes:

> As difficult as this may be to digest, the ideology which stands for fail-ure, suffering and death, and has shown nothing but contempt for all humanity, still possesses the capacity to represent itself as good, fair, loving and caring. This is why it is urgent to clear away the layers of misconception and disinformation which have come to hide the true foundations of so-called Liberalism in America.

Like many who've emigrated to America after witnessing socialism firsthand, Mr. Vazsonyi was appalled to see America following the same disastrous course—a course that had all but destroyed Europe.

Socialism is, at bottom, a secularization of the ethics of religion—an ethics that views man as morally depraved and therefore in need of guidance by the "enlightened." If humans are "radically evil," said Kant, democracy is not for them, but for angels. Humans will have to be "forced to be free" by the Enlighteners, said Rousseau.

Jefferson saw things differently than Kant and Rousseau:

> Sometimes it is said that man cannot be trusted with the government of himself. Can he, then, be trusted with the government of others? Or have we found angels in the form of kings to govern him? Let history answer this question.

Now, the question that matters here—in this divided country with this alleged "debate" between Democrats and Republicans—is this: is this a really a debate about two different interpretations of the American philosophy? Or are we in the midst of a much larger battle between the original American philosophy and something else entirely?

In fact, are we really having a debate in this country at all or are we fighting a mental virus?

As mentioned previously, the "other thing," the alien philosophy that has infected Americans and take us away from the original American construct, is socialism.

Like a hydra-headed monster, socialism and collectivism come in various guises, which we can refer to under the broad category of Statism. Apparently it doesn't matter how many times we chop off a head, new ones keep growing.

However, the common principle is the same: the sacrifice of the individual to a society or a god.

The common method is the same: some men claim special knowledge about what "god" or "society" demands of all men and the others must obey, through force if necessary.

And the common end result is the same: mass poverty, mass suffering, and mass oppression.

In America, what we have been dealing with for the past one hundred years at least, is collectivism of the secular (socialist-communist-fascist) variety, with the lion's share of the credit going to Karl Marx and his followers.

"To be a socialist," said the Nazi leader Goebbels, "is to submit the I to the thou; socialism is sacrificing the individual to the whole."

The New Socialists' Game

The socialists of today do not, of course, advocate violence on the scale of a Lenin or a Hitler. They are much more sophisticated than that. They are into "soft tyranny" and incrementalism.

Their game goes like this…

First, they segment society into "groups" with supposedly conflicting interests, such as rich vs. poor; labor vs. management; black vs. white, men vs. women, Wall Street vs. Main Street, capitalists vs. environmentalists.

Then they set themselves up as the crusaders for, and arbiters of, "social justice," "fairness," and "rights." They are the champions of the "needy" and "the little guy" and "the working man" and the "oppressed." They seek to transform America from a success-oriented society into a problem-oriented society. They trot out victim parades in order to prove their case.

They then re-write history and cast aspersions on our traditional heroes (read Howard Zinn or Noam Chomsky for example). They harp on the few flaws and ignore the overwhelming good.

As Professor C. Bradley Thompson, author of John Adams and The Spirit of Liberty, puts it…

> There was a time when American schoolchildren were required to study the great events, the wise statesmen, the courageous warriors, the brilliant inventors, and the ingenious industrialists of American history. There was a time when American students knew, in great detail the heroic story of the American Revolution and the tragedy of the Civil War

Today, our children are being taught to be ashamed of America. By denigrating the principles and great deeds of America's past and dethroning its heroes, today's college professors are destroying in our youth the proper reverence for the ideals this nation stands for. And a nation that hates itself cannot last.

After tearing down our heroes and evading the greatness of America, socialists then seek to equalize by "re-distributing" between groups they manufacture in their imaginations—from the "oppressors" to the "oppressed," from the rich to the poor, from the politically incorrect to the politically correct. As the Communist motto goes "from each according to his ability; to each according to his need." That saying should send chills up the spine of anyone who truly loves freedom.

Next, taking their cues from Rousseau and Kant, they begin to use the machinery of Government legislation to force people to abide by their socialist ideas and conform to their vision of the world.

Ability is sacrificed to need.

Individual rights are violated in the name of "fairness."

Property rights are violated in the name of "redistribution of wealth."

Private property (such as office places and restaurants) becomes "public" property.

Free speech is sacrificed to "political correctness."

Producers and achievers become greedy "exploiters."

The rights of humans are sacrificed to the alleged rights of animals, rocks, and trees.

And what of Liberty? What of America's most sacred founding principle?

Liberty is not even the slightest concern of our self-anointed champions of social justice.

After all, says this mindset, what does it matter if a millionaire earned his money honestly through his own hard work and ability? It's not "fair" that he has all that money while so many people are in need. All that selfish so-and-so cares about is "money," while we care about "the people."

Sound familiar?

Why Socialism Makes Politics Personal

Socialism makes politics personal because socialism and all forms of statism are based on force.

If we had a free society based in Liberty, then politics would not be nearly as personal as it is today because neither individuals nor groups of Americans would have the right to force their opinions on others and redistribute income through government legislation. The problem is some of us continue to advocate the principle of liberty but a huge percentage of Americans do not. They say "there ought to be a law" at the drop of a hat. Naturally, when a person is advocating that the government takes hard-earned money from your family and spends it on things you consider none of the government's business, disagree with, or even abhor, that is something to take personally.

This type of redistribution is always smuggled in under the guise of compassion and concern for the "needy." However, the premise that we need the government to take care of the truly needy in society—through enforced taxation—is false. The history of America shows that picking your neighbors pockets by way of politicians is not a necessity for survival.

Although capitalism had just begun to flourish in the 19th century, the vast majority of Americans were already able to support themselves through their own productive work. Only a tiny sliver of a minority depended on assistance and aid. That aid was NOT provided by the government, yet there was no shortage of aid for those that truly needed it.

"Those in need," historian Walter Trattner writes in his book From Poor Law to The Welfare State, ". . . looked first to family, kin, and neighbors for aid, including the landlord, who sometimes deferred the rent; the local butcher or grocer, who frequently carried them for a while by allowing bills to go unpaid; and the local saloonkeeper, who often came to their aid by providing loans and outright gifts, including free meals and, on occasion, temporary jobs. Next, the needy sought assistance from various agencies in the community–those of their own devising, such as churches or religious groups, social and fraternal associations, mutual aid societies, local ethnic groups, and trade unions."

The "mutual aid" societies that existed were organizations that let people insure against a variety of things that our modern "entitlement" programs now claim to address. However, these societies were not charities and there was no government involvement. Those who joined would voluntarily pay membership dues in return for a defined schedule of benefits, which could include things like life insurance, disability insurance, sickness and accident benefits, old-age benefits, and funeral benefits. These societies were private and had a wide range of options to fit a wide range of needs. And of course, they were voluntary, so people only joined if they made sense for them.

These groups were abundant in the late 19th and early 20th centuries. In 1910, for instance, New York State had 151 private benevolent groups providing care for children, and 216 providing care for adults or adults with children. If you were down on your luck or homeless in Chicago in 1933, you could find shelter at one of the city's 614 YMCAs, one of its 89 Salvation Army barracks, or one of its 75 Goodwill Industries dormitories.

"In fact," writes Trattner, "so rapidly did private agencies multiply that before long America's larger cities had what to many people was an embarrassing number of them. Charity directories took as many as 100 pages to list and describe the numerous voluntary agencies that sought to alleviate misery, and combat every imaginable emergency."

Today, in our hyper-connected, social media driven society, it would be even easier to facilitate organizations and private charities along the same lines. The idea that we need the government to provide a "safety net" is simply not true and we pay a tremendous price for buying into that lie.

However, we won't get rid of the entitlement state until we get rid of the entitlement mentality… and our politicians are not exactly helping with that cause.

Singing to Karl Marx's Tune

During every American Presidential election, we hear the same tired refrains, with politicians singing to Karl Marx's tune…

"The rich should pay their fair share of taxes," "universal health care for all," "free college for every child," "raise the minimum wage," "spread the wealth," "end tax cuts for the rich," and on and on. It's all pure demagoguery based on an immoral philosophy and flat out lies about its efficacy. Politicians prey on the emotions of the electorate as well as their ignorance of political philosophy, basic economics, and our founding ideals.

There is something truly obscene about career politicians and limousine liberals, many of whom were born into wealth and privilege, railing against tax cuts for the "rich" and vilifying business owners and entrepreneurs (producers) as exploiters. Many of them such as Mr. Obama do it at fundraising dinners that cost $35,000 a plate. What's wrong with this picture?

Many of the shrillest politicians have never had to work a day in their life, so perhaps they don't appreciate how difficult it is to actually earn your living. Most do not have the slightest clue as to what it takes to start and run a productive enterprise. All they know is businesses and the "rich" have the money so they have to denigrate them and portray them as evil in order to loot them (for the purpose of buying votes) without feeling guilty.

Don't fall for the socialist line that "Republicans only care about money, while we compassionate Democrats care about the people." That is the oldest and most transparent socialist cliché in the book. It's an attempt by enemies of Liberty to gain the moral high ground by claiming they are "humanitarians"—just before they stick a gun to your head.

This view of government as Robin Hood, or a social welfare agency, ignores two important facts:

1. Taking money from someone without their consent is stealing. That is immoral. It does not matter how much money the victim has, and it does

not matter if the proceeds are used for an allegedly “good purpose.” If I rob Peter and give the money to Paul, that does not make me generous. It makes me a thief. A rich man has the same inalienable rights to his property as do I. People rationalize this by saying, “well, it’s the government that is doing it and these politicians were democratically elected so it’s ok.” No, it’s not ok in the context of the original American system or the values of a free society—the government possesses no rights that we ourselves don’t possess individually. If I don’t have a right to make my neighbor pay my Health Care premiums neither does the government.

2. Throwing other people’s money at so-called social problems has “such a miserable track record of failure that only an intellectual could evade or ignore it,” as Economist Thomas Sowell says. The modern welfare state is an unmitigated disaster. If we continue to expand it, we are heading down the same road as Soviet Russia, just at a slower pace. The Communists were just Socialists in a hurry.

Our current President, Barack Obama, is a particularly smooth snake oil salesman and he’s been able to pull the wool over the eyes of many. He’s the latest in a long line of socialist messiahs that is going to lead the masses to the promised land. The amazing fact is he didn’t even hide his far left views as liberal politicians have always had to do in the past. Incredibly, his long time associations with former terrorists such as Bill Ayers, and racist, America-hating Preachers such as Jeremiah Wright, seemed to just roll off the backs of much of the electorate—an electorate that was apparently full of misplaced white guilt and more interested in skin pigmentation than in the substance of ideas and policies.

Many have been surprised at the unmitigated disaster that his Presidency has been. They have been shocked by his record-setting deficits and the fact that he’s grown the national debt by $5 trillion in just three short years. But why is anyone surprised? He showed everyone clearly what he was since the very beginning of his run for President.

In campaign interviews and speeches, he even had the audacity to use lines such as in the following examples…

In an interview with commentator Bill O’Reilly, he said the following when O’Reilly asked him why he wanted to raise taxes: “look Bill, you’re well off, so if we take some money from you and give it to a waitress, that’s just being neighborly.”

Neighborly?

To the famous "Joe the Plumber," he said, "I'm not trying to punish you for your success; we're just trying to spread the wealth around so people behind you can succeed too."

Marx could not have said it better.

In November, 2007, at a campaign rally in Durham, NC, he said the following, "We've got to make sure that people who have more money help the people who have less money. If you had a whole pizza, and your friend had no pizza, would you give him a slice?"

Boy does he think Americans are dumb. Are we?

On the campaign stump in 2008, when questioned about his plan to raise taxes for those earning over $200,000, he said, "since when did we want to make a virtue out of selfishness?..."

I see, so if you work hard and actually want to keep your own money for your own family you are "selfish." And according to Mr. Obama, being "selfish" is a very bad thing—so he will force you to be "unselfish."

In his book, *The Audacity Of Hope*, he says this, "Billionaires have this idea that it's their money and they deserve to keep every penny of it."

Maybe he should have called it, *The Audacity of Socialism*. Apparently it's not their money, and Mr. Obama will tell them how much they can keep (and it won't be much).

In other words, in all the examples above, what he is saying is this: "when we come to take even more of your hard-earned money... so we can spend it however we see fit, waste it wherever we want, and give it to the groups that voted for me but did not earn it... If you object and tell me that you'd prefer to keep it for yourself and your children, you are just not being 'neighborly.' You are preventing others from succeeding. You're just being 'selfish.' Therefore we will need to take it from you by force."

That is all pure socialism and it is perverse. It is the opposite of freedom and the antithesis of everything this country was founded on.

When you see Mr. Obama say things like that, do you understand it is socialism and rebel against it in principle? Do you understand how evil it is?

True to form, now that he's President, Mr. Obama is pursuing a full-scale socialist agenda, with massive government spending, borrowing, regulating, dictating and taxing. He has already driven us off the cliff straight into financial oblivion.

Given everything we learned about him during the campaign that was all entirely predictable.

Socialism is a philosophy of failure, the creed of ignorance, and the gospel of envy, its inherent virtue is the equal sharing of misery.

— Winston Churchill

Allow me to make one more point in this chapter to further illustrate the difference between a political operator like Mr. Obama, and a man of integrity and achievement, who actually creates values as well as livelihoods for others (like inventors, scientists, doctors, entrepreneurs and businessmen).

During the campaign, conservatives rightly pointed out that Mr. Obama's only experience prior to running for office was the dubious distinction of being a "community organizer." Democrats shot back that he "helped" people in the community after a steel plant closed down.

How did he help them exactly? Did he risk his own capital? Did he invest his own money, time, energy and efforts to organize and open a new steel plant, or a new manufacturing facility to provide the laid off workers with jobs? That is something that would have truly helped the community, would it not?

No, of course he didn't do that. His "helping" took the form of trying to get "other people's money," through coercive tactics, in order to give it to the laid off workers for short-term needs, retraining, etc. To the extent he achieved anything, they were not the achievements of a producer; they were the achievements of a shakedown artist.

However, Barack Obama is not the problem. The problem is we now live in a country where someone like Barack Obama can be elected President. "We the people" have become the problem and we are getting the politicians we deserve.

In order not to be sucked in by posturing politicians, every American must have a clear understanding of how the ideas behind political policies shape our society; so let's take a closer look at our two competing political ideologies—Capitalism and Socialism—and see the results of following each course in practice.

CHAPTER 4
CAPITALISM VS. SOCIALISM

How fine the world would be if the State were free to cure all ills! It is one step only from such a mentality to the perfect totalitarianism of Stalin and Hitler. – Ludwig von Mises

Essentially, what today's politicians believe is that government is supposed to solve all of the problems in society (real or imagined) through its coercive power. The fact that they actually think they can or should do that, is what Economist Frederick Hayek called the "fatal conceit" that led to the Totalitarian states of the 20th century. However, politicians never seem to learn from history. Because they don't, they condemn the rest of us to repeat it.

It's not just the politicians of course. A vast number of our citizens believe that is the role of government as well. By calling for laws and regulations that are outside the scope of protecting individual rights, they propose to use the machinery of government to force their opinions and views on other people (no matter how dubious or flat out wrong). The current call for regulation of CO2 production due to the global warming hoax and the PowerPoint presentation by the eminent scientist Al Gore is a prime example.

Look at the front page of any major newspaper, and you will see the same familiar pattern. You first read about some sort of "crisis" that is happening or could happen. As you read the article, it will become clear that the writer of the article believes that the government should be the entity that somehow provides the solution for the alleged crisis or problem.

As the great journalist, H.L. Mencken wrote, "The whole aim of practical politics is to keep the populace alarmed (and hence clamorous to be led to safety) by menacing it with an endless series of hobgoblins, all of them imaginary." Unfortunately, the majority of those who write and report in the mainstream media are nothing more than government lackeys today. True journalism of the kind Mencken practiced is dead.

Those who advocate an activist government believe that Liberty may be violated, if such violation serves a "greater good," as defined by whoever is clamoring for the government intervention of course. That's the opposite of what America's Founding Fathers believed.

It is what Marx and Lenin and Hitler believed however.

It should be noted, that unlike those who value liberty, socialists do not settle for using mere logic, facts, and persuasion to turn others around to their way of thinking. They do it by force, using the government as their proxy. As Buckminster Fuller noted, "the end move of a socialist is always to reach for a gun."

There is a reason for that. Due to our heritage and our "sense of life," most Americans still, at least on an emotional level, value liberty and freedom and have the common sense not to fall for socialist nonsense when it is presented for what it is. Instead of envying the rich, we believe that if we work hard enough, and provide enough value to our fellow men, we can become rich too if that's our goal. Instead of looking for handouts, we believe in taking responsibility for ourselves and meeting our own needs.

This positive sense of life, this "spirit of enterprise," has produced the famous inventors and entrepreneurs of our history… men like Thomas Edison, Commodore Vanderbilt, Andrew Carnegie, Henry Ford, The Wright Brothers, John D. Rockefeller, James Roebling, James J. Hill, Thomas Watson, Bill Gates, Steve Jobs, Andy Grove and countless more—the productive geniuses of American history that drove the world forward and raised up everyone in their wake.

Any one of the above individuals has produced far more benefits for their fellow man than all of the social workers, posturing politicians, and Mother Theresas in human history put together!

They have done it through the inventions, products, services, jobs, technological innovations, and vast industries they created.

James J. Hill is a good example. Although his father died when he was fourteen and he had to drop out of school and work as a grocery clerk to support his widowed mother, James J. Hill almost single handedly opened the American northwest….

Building A Railroad

Most historians assume that the transcontinental railroad system could not have been built without government subsidies. It is true that the Union Pacific and the Central Pacific, completed in the years after the Civil War, received per-mile subsidies from the government in the form of land grants and low-interest loans. But was this federal funding necessary? Of course not. James J. Hill proved that railroads could be built privately just as many private roads and canals were built using private financing in the early 19th century. Despite having to compete with competitors that were subsidized by the government, James J. Hill built the Great Northern railroad without any government aid whatsoever.

Hill naturally opposed favors to his competitors, writing, "The government should not furnish capital to these companies, in addition to their enormous land subsidies, to enable them to conduct their business in competition with enterprises that have received no aid from the public treasury."

Despite having to compete with government funded railroads, Hill built the Great Northern into the best constructed and most profitable of all the major railroads. In fact, Hill's Great Northern was the only trans-continental railroad that never went bankrupt.

While the government subsidized railroads were built quickly and shoddily since they were being paid on a per-mile of track basis, not on the basis of profitability, Hill had to turn a profit and pay his way in cash. Under his direction, his workers laid rail twice as fast as his competitors but maintained higher quality. He was obsessive about cutting waste and passed any cost cutting on to his customers in the form of lower rates. Knowing how harsh the Northwest winters were, he used the best quality materials even if they were more expensive.

He also knew that those who used his rail services—including timber companies, miners, and farmers—would succeed or fail along with him. He worked to improve the prosperity of the people along the lines of his railroad in a number of ways. He provided free seed grain to farmers along with educational materials about crop diversification. He donated land to the communities along his lines for parks, schools and churches. He transported immigrants to the Great Plains for low rates if they promised to farm near his rail lines. His motto to the people of the Northwest was this, "We have to prosper with you or we have got to be poor with you." All of this generated goodwill, had the communities pulling for him, and was also good for business.

In a biography of Hill, Burton Fulsom describes his compulsion for excellence:

> Hill's quest for short routes, low grades, and few curvatures was an obsession. In 1889 Hill conquered the Rocky Mountains by finding the legendary Maria Pass. Lewis and Clark had described a low pass through the Rockies back in 1805; but later no one seemed to know whether it really existed or, if it did, where it was. Hill wanted the best gradient so much that he hired a man to spend months searching the western Montana for the pass. He did in fact find it, and the ecstatic Hill shortened his route by almost one hundred miles.

Hill's railroad went on to be a great success and he later got into the steamship business, selling American exports to the Orient. He also got into the timber business with his partner Frederick Weyerhaeuser, selling Northwest timber to other parts of the country.

However, despite the fact that he had to succeed against government-subsidized competitors, Hill was unfairly lumped in with "businessmen" who were really political operators and became the victim of the Interstate Commerce Act of 1887. This Act was supposed to ban "rate rail discrimination," making it illegal to charge different rates to different customers. What the Act did was force every railroad owner to charge everyone the same high rates (supposedly in the name of "consumer protection."). This hurt Hill badly because he was the most vigorous price discounter. Worse, like all government interventions into the private sector, the Act came with a bureaucratic monstrosity called the Interstate Commerce Commission, which soon attempted to manage and control all aspects of the railroad business, hampering its efficiency even further. This effectively put him out of business.

Years later, reflecting on his accomplishments and how he had to fight politicians every step of the way, Hill said this:

> It really seems hard when we look back at what we have done and how we have led all western companies in opening the country... that we should be compelled to fight for our lives against political adventurers who have never done anything but pose and draw a salary.
>
> — James Jerome Hill

Since we're talking about American Ideals, it's important to note that men like James J. Hill, and all other great entrepreneurs, did not do what they did out of altruism—they did it out of a desire to achieve their own goals and values in life. They made the most of their unalienable rights to life and liberty and pursued their own happiness. Most of these men started with nothing. That is a phenomenon that can only happen in a free society. To this day, eighty-percent of the millionaires in America are "self-made," or first generation affluent.

In speaking about the individual nature of entrepreneurship and achievement, the late Steve Jobs, who is likely the greatest creator and entrepreneur of our time, put it this way in his 2005 Commencement address at Stanford...

> We think the Mac will sell zillions, but we didn't build the Mac for anybody else. We built it for ourselves. We were the group of people who were going to judge whether it was

> great or not. We weren't going to go out and do market research. We just wanted to build the best thing we could build.
>
> When you're a carpenter making a beautiful chest of drawers, you're not going to use a piece of plywood on the back, even though it faces the wall and nobody will ever see it. You'll know it's there, so you're going to use a beautiful piece of wood on the back. For you to sleep well at night, the aesthetic, the quality, has to be carried all the way through.

And he comments further on what it means to live life on your own terms, not a "second hand" life driven by someone else's agenda:

Your time is limited, so don't waste it living someone else's life. Don't be trapped by dogma — which is living with the results of other people's thinking. Don't let the noise of others' opinions drown out your own inner voice. And most important, have the courage to follow your heart and intuition. They somehow already know what you truly want to become. Everything else is secondary.

To take one more example, Warren Brookes, in his book, The Economy in Mind, tells a relevant story about the Kimberly Clark Corporation and its founder, Ernst Mahler…

> Mahler was an entrepreneurial genius, whose innovative ideas and leadership, over a period of about 20 years, transformed [Kimberly Clark, a] once-small, insular newsprint and tissue manufacturer into one of the largest paper corporations in the world, which gives prosperous employment to more than 100,000 and produces products (which Mahler helped to innovate) that are now used by more than 2 billion people. Mahler became enormously wealthy, of course. Yet his personal fortune was insignificant when compared with the permanent prosperity he generated, not only for his own company but for the hundreds of thousands who work for industries which his genius ultimately spawned and which long outlived him. I can safely predict that you have never heard of him up to this moment. Not one person in 100 million has. Yet his contribution has permanently uplifted the lives of millions and far exceeds in real compassion most of our self-congratulatory politicians and "activists" whose names are known to all.

One could fill volumes with such examples.

Since the fall of the Berlin wall, most of the world understands the benefits of capitalism also. People in countries that were formerly mired in statism, such as India and China, are beginning to break their ancient chains and benefit from elements of freedom and capitalism for the first time. Eastern European states like the Czech Republic, formerly crushed under the iron heel of communism, understand it also.

In the past three decades, an orientation toward free markets and capitalism has been steadily improving much of the world that was formerly oppressed… yet our own political demagogues still cling to their tired old Marxist rhetoric and want to pull us back down into the pit of socialism and class warfare. Why?

Tragically, despite its profound successes over the past two hundred years, there is still resistance against Capitalism in the United States. We currently have a "mixed" economy that is now more than half socialist. And whether we want to face it or not, we have been moving in one direction consistently for the past century—and that direction is away from capitalism and toward statism.

If we're ever going to put the brakes on and move in the right direction, it's important to be clear about what capitalism is and why it is the only socio-economic system consistent with Liberty.

Capitalism Is Based On Individual Rights

Capitalism is more than just an economic system. As Ayn Rand put it, "Capitalism is a social system based on the recognition of individual rights, including property rights, in which all property is privately owned." This includes tangible property (like land) and intangible property (like ideas). Capitalism is the system that protects the inalienable right of each individual to his or her own life and liberty.

When individual rights are properly protected by the government, men must get what they want from each other by trading, rather than looting. They must deal with each other in terms of value exchanges, as opposed to power exchanges. They must offer something of value for money and convince the other party that what they offer is worth more than the money the other person will pay for the service or product.

By each person acting in his own self-interest, based on his own free judgment, the result is a win-win exchange in which both sides benefit from the trade or transaction. Most importantly, in a capitalist system, men must deal with each other peacefully and enforce agreements through mutually agreed upon contracts, rather than by using force and compulsion.

Moreover, a social system that protects individual rights, protects rights beyond the scope of economic rights as well—including freedom of speech, freedom of the press, freedom of religion, the right to voluntary association and the right to vote.

In other words, Capitalism is a social system based on Liberty, Freedom, and Justice.

This is precisely why Capitalism works so well—because it is a system of freedom and rational self-interest, both of which are consistent with and required by man's nature.

In 1776, the same year the American Colonies declared their

independence, Adam Smith published a book called *The Wealth Of Nations*. This was the first great treatise on capitalism. In it, Smith noted…

> In civilized society he [man] stands at all times in need of the cooperation and assistance of great multitudes, while his whole life is scarce sufficient to gain the friendship of a few persons. In almost every other race of animals each individual, when it is grown up to maturity, is entirely independent, and in its natural state has occasion for the assistance of no other living creature. But man has almost constant occasion for the help of his brethren, and it is in vain for him to expect it from their benevolence only. He will be more likely to prevail if he can interest their self-love in his favour, and show them that it is for their own advantage to do for him what he requires of them. Whoever offers to another a bargain of any kind, proposes to do this. Give me that which I want, and you shall have this which you want, is the meaning of every offer; and it is in this manner that we obtain from one another the far greater part of those good offices which we stand in need of. It is not from the benevolence of the butcher, the brewer, or the baker that we expect our dinner, but from their regard to their self-love, and never talk to them of our own necessities but of their advantages.

Like the consumers that he sells to, the entrepreneur acts in his own self-interest. He creates his products and services in order to make money, to care for his loved ones, to enjoy life, to build wealth, and for the love of achievement and excellence as so aptly stated by Steve Jobs in the quotes above. The only way a businessman can get rich is by providing competitive values to his fellow human beings on a massive scale. He must provide the consumer he sells to with benefits that they perceive as being greater than their cost. And he must do it profitably within the context of a rapidly changing, competitive environment.

Accomplishing that is incredibly difficult. In fact, studies consistently show that only 2 out of every 10 new businesses started in the U.S. survive for even three years. When entrepreneurs and corporations succeed on a large scale, by building a large and successful company, they should be praised, not vilified. The payments they receive personally, no matter how large, will always be a fraction of the value they have provided to "society" and those they employ. The business owners that earn the most profits through honest dealings are the ones that have produced the greatest value to their fellow men. That is moral and good, not at all exploitative.

It's important here to note here that we're talking about businessmen who compete openly and honestly in the free market, and not "political" businessmen who seek unearned advantages through government "pull" and favors from politicians. Political entrepreneurs have always been around. They were the ones who ran the government-subsidized railroads in James J. Hill's time. This is a phenomenon we are seeing more and more of today in the wake of the unprecedented bailouts and government takeovers in the banking and auto industries.

The easiest way to solve the problem of "political" businessmen, sometimes referred to as crony capitalism, is simply to enforce a strict separation of economics and state, i.e., get the government out of regulating business and therefore being in the position of granting favors. In other words, if you want to get the money out of politics, get the politics out of making money.

Think about it—why should men who produce nothing have any control whatsoever over the men who produce everything? Why should someone like James J. Hill have had to answer to know-nothing bureaucrats at the Inter-state Commerce Commission?

Real Capitalism vs. a "Mixed Economy"

To be clear, when we talk about capitalism as a social system, we are talking about actual capitalism, or laissez-faire capitalism. The French term "laissez-nous faire" means "leave us be," meaning the government should not interfere in the marketplace.

The first recorded use of the "laissez-faire" maxim was by French minister René de Voyer, Marquis d'Argenson, another champion of free trade, in his famous outburst:

> Let them be, such should be the motto of every public authority, according to which the world is civilized.... A detestable principle that which would not wish us to grow except by lowering our neighbors! There is nothing but mischief and malignity of heart in those satisfied with that principle, and interest is opposed to it. Leave them be, damn it! Leave them be!

It is a "detestable principle" indeed, which "would not wish us to grow except by lowering our neighbors," yet that is the principle of socialism and the motive force behind our current political era.

Let me note a point here to clarify thinking. When we talk about laissez-faire capitalism operating on the basis of the profit motive, that presupposes an ethical environment. The same laws against force and fraud that apply to individuals apply to businesses operating under a free market system. In addition, it is in the entrepreneur's interest to protect his reputation for providing value and dealing honestly, or else he will not be in business for long and may even be ostracized from the business community for good.

Statists will often try to portray capitalism as "the wild west," where greedy businessmen operate without any laws or restrictions and exploit "the little people." That's a dishonest portrayal and not even remotely the case.

What laissez-faire does mean is that businessmen can operate without politicians constantly throwing sand in their gears, tying them up with mountains of paperwork, choking their ability to make a profit through regulations, and generally hampering their growth and ability to innovate. Politicians claim constitutional powers to do this by citing the Interstate Commerce clause from the Constitution.

The Interstate Commerce clause, which was first wielded against James J. Hill and has been used to bludgeon and bedevil businesses ever since, was not intended by the Founders to be used in the way it is now being used. It was NOT intended to "regulate" in our modern sense of the term (i.e, dictate and control). In fact, the original intention was just the opposite. In the 18th century "regulate" meant "to make regular," i.e., to standardize. It was inserted by the Framers of the Constitution in an attempt to remove the varying and burdensome laws that each state had at the time because they were slowing down commerce and trade between the states. In other words, the intent of the commerce clause was simply to remove barriers to interstate trade.

The Great Economists on Capitalism

By any honest measure, the greatest free market economist of the 20th century has to be Ludwig von Mises. In over six decades of work, Mises showed that the only viable economic policy for the human race was a policy of unrestricted laissez-faire capitalism, or free markets that protected the right of private property, with government strictly limited to the defense of person and property.

In other words, he agreed fully with America's Founding Fathers. However, because he was an economist, and not a politician, he was mainly concerned with the study of economics as a science. His key insight was that the whole economy is the result of what individuals do; it is based on "human action" for the purpose of achieving desired goals.

As early as 1922, in his book, Socialism, Mises predicted what would happen to Europe if it continued on its socialistic path. Had people heeded Mises warnings then, the world would have avoided the Great Depression as well as European totalitarianism and the subsequent world war. But Europe did not heed Mises, and the darkness of national socialism came to Germany. When the Nazis took over Austria, Mises escaped and came to America, where he had a great influence on free market economics.

Mises not only showed why government intervention would inevitably lead to depressions, he demonstrated that socialism would be disastrous for a modern economy because the absence of private ownership of land and capital goods prevents any sort of rational pricing, or estimate of costs. He showed that government intervention, in addition to hampering and crippling the market, would prove counter-productive and feed on itself, leading inevitably to socialism unless the entire web of interventions was repealed.

In his magnum opus, *Human Action*, Mises neatly summarizes the difference between political power and economic power, pointing out that the consumer is the true "captain" of the free market economy:

> All that good government can do to improve the material well-being of the masses is to establish and to preserve an institutional setting in which there are no obstacles to the progressive accumulation of new capital and its utilization for the improvement of technical methods of production ... The direction of all economic affairs in the market society is a task of the entrepreneurs. Theirs is the control of production. They are at the helm and steer the ship. A superficial observer would believe that they are supreme. But they are not. They are bound to obey unconditionally the captain's orders. The captain is the consumer. Consumers make poor people rich and rich people poor. They determine precisely what should be produced, in what quality, and in what quantities.

Mises' student, F.A. von Hayek wrote, "Capitalism is not only a better form of organizing human activity than any deliberate design… it is also the indispensable condition for just keeping that population alive which exists already in the world. I regard the preservation of what is known as the capitalist system, of the system of free markets and the private ownership of the means of production, as an essential condition of the very survival of mankind. ... Perhaps the fact that we have seen millions voting themselves into complete dependence on a tyrant has made our generation understand that to choose one's government is not necessarily to secure freedom. ... Emergencies' have always been the pretext on which the safeguards of individual liberty have been eroded."

Precisely. That's why in the wake of 2008's "October Surprise" (the catastrophic meltdown of the nation's largest financial institutions), President Obama's chief of staff, Rahm Emanuel, said of their strategy: "Rule 1: Never allow a crisis to go to waste. They are opportunities to do big things." Yes, in the view of people like Emanuel and Obama, the big thing they want to do is "fundamentally transform" America from a capitalist country into a socialist country.

Perhaps the best known economist of the last century was Milton Friedman, author of *Free to Choose*. Friedman wrote, "The Great

Depression, like most other periods of severe unemployment, was produced by government mismanagement rather than by any inherent instability of the private economy. Roosevelt's policies were very destructive. Roosevelt's policies made the depression longer and worse than it otherwise would have been."

As a fascinating aside, today's Federal Reserve Chairman, Ben Bernanke, admitted this in 2002, after summarizing a 1963 book by Freidman and Anna Schwartz. "As an official representative of the Federal Reserve," said Bernanke. "I would like to say to Milton and Anna, regarding the Great Depression: You're right, we did it. We're very sorry. But thanks to you, we won't do it again. " Unfortunately, this admission by Bernanke did nothing to change the Fed's monetary policies.

Another great Economist of the 20th century, Henry Hazlitt, summed up Capitalism very nicely in a way that dovetails with the Founding Fathers sentiments…

> Capitalism may be thought of as a combination of two institutions—private property and the free market. Private property means that everyone is free to keep the fruits of his labor, or to put them to any use he sees fit, as long as he does not infringe the similar rights of others.
>
> — Henry Hazlitt

Socialism Is Based On Force and Coercion

Socialism can very simply be defined as "society owning or controlling the means of production." Since "society" as such doesn't exist, only individuals exist, what this amounts to in practice is certain individuals in the government controlling and exploiting everyone else. What this leads to is class warfare and economic cannibalism. Under socialism, our fellow citizens are no longer seen as free and sovereign individuals, whose rights we need to respect. They become seen as either "resources" to plunder on the one hand, or "looters" who are intent on taking from us on the other.

> Socialism is not a movement of the people. It is a movement of the intellectuals, originated, led and controlled by the intellectuals, carried by them out of their stuffy ivory towers into those bloody fields of practice where they unite with their allies and executors: the thugs.
>
> — Ayn Rand, "The Monument Builders", 1962

That is not how it should be in America. Most thinking Americans understand that feudalism and class warfare ended when the concept of Liberty was enshrined in our Constitution and was further obliterated by the Industrial Revolution and Capitalism.

They understand that businessmen are not greedy "exploiters," but risk takers, inventors, and producers, providing an ever-increasing array of valuable products and services that simultaneously fill human wants and needs and also create livelihoods for millions of human beings as they too take part in the process of value production. Ultimately, entrepreneurs are value creators.

But even Americans can be fooled for a while—and they have been fooled for several decades now. The reason they have been fooled is because socialism comes dressed up as something else…

Socialists (modern liberals) play to the American sense of fairness and equality, for their concern for the underdog and the "little guy." Socialist intellectuals have a remarkable ability to pervert language and vocabulary for their purposes. This is especially true in America. At least in Europe socialists still have the decency to call themselves by that name. However, in America socialism has always been a tougher sell, so socialists used other terms such as "progressive," and even co-opted the term liberal which used to mean the opposite of socialism in its classical use!

As Norman Thomas, a six-time Presidential candidate of the American socialist party, famously said…

> The American people will never knowingly adopt Socialism. But under the name of 'liberalism' they will adopt every fragment of the Socialist program, until one day America will be a Socialist nation, without knowing how it happened.

Unfortunately, Mr. Thomas was extremely prescient.

Another example of how socialists manipulate language is the concept of "equality." Socialists turn it on its ear. Where it once meant equality before the law, and that each man is equally free to pursue his own happiness, it now becomes equality of results or "outcome." This turns the pursuit of happiness into "other people owe me happiness."

The goal of equality under this meaning is supposedly "fairness," and that each person is entitled to an "equal slice of the pie." Statists fail to understand the most basic truth about economics and wealth creation—it is not a zero sum game. First of all, there is no pie. The pie has to be created. Then, once it's created, the so-called pie is not of a fixed size nor does someone have a right to a piece simply because they want one—they have to work for it and earn it, otherwise they should go and create their own pies.

But even more importantly, freedom and capitalism make these pies grow, and capitalism also keeps creating new and better pies! Socialists and modern liberals do not understand that. Their brains are frozen with a primitive scarcity mentality rather than an abundance mentality. They don't understand that wealth is created. They think there's a finite sum out there, controlled by greedy people, and they just need to grab their share by force and move it around however they see fit (while taking a big heap off the top for themselves of course).

This false idea that economics is a zero sum game and wealth does not need to be created is one of the many legacies of Karl Marx. Marx is actually the one who coined the term "capitalism," ostensibly to use it as an insult against those focused on capital, or money, vs. the needs of society. Marx's basic theory was presented in a document presented by himself and Frederich Engels of just forty pages, called *The Communist Manifesto*. (It's a shame it wasn't a lot longer, because then few people would have read it.)

This "manifesto" makes some attempt to explain the economic theories of Communism, but its main purpose was to work as a propaganda tool, a call for civil war: "Working men of all countries, unite!"

Marx's economic theory was based on the idea that business owners exploited the workers. He offers no explanation of the extent of that exploitation, nor does he provide any evidence of how this was possible since employers could not use force. But that doesn't really matter, all if it was pure fiction. Socialism is about gaining political power and control.

Henry Hazlitt cuts to the chase in explaining the main thrust of the forty pages of Marx's "manifesto…"

> We are told that there are two main classes in society—the "proletariat," which consists of the "workers," employed and unemployed, and forms allegedly about nine-tenths of the population, and the "bourgeoisie," which consists of the employers and a few other groups who are comfortably well off. The bourgeoisie rule. They hire the proletariat; and because they do, they necessarily "exploit" them. The only way this dreadful situation can be changed is by revolution, in which the proletariat must seize all the property of the bourgeoisie, and, if they object, kill them.

Marxism can be viewed as a rather primitive critique of feudalism (which was based on force), but it has no relevance whatsoever to a society based on individual rights and organized around free market capitalism.

It is free trade, production and wealth creation that are the essence of capitalism, and this has been demonstrated in dramatic fashion over the past 200 years. But no matter how great the progress, no matter how many people are lifted out of poverty, there are those who attack the producers and wealth creators.

What are the motivations of anti-capitalists? There are many. Some do it out of economic ignorance… some out of a desire for power…. some out of unearned guilt…. some out of self-loathing and envy… some out of a sincere but misguided desire to improve the human condition. One recurring theme is the one of "fairness," or egalitarianism.

Egalitarianism

One aspect of socialism that many liberals promote is egalitarianism and, interestingly enough, it has its roots in the French revolution. Unlike the American Revolution, the French Revolution was followed by a bloody slaughter and "Reign of Terror." Why? Because, while the American Revolution was about securing Liberty, the French revolution sought to enforce "equality." Essentially, what it did was overthrow feudalism with dictatorship.

Whereas the American Revolution resulted in the individual becoming sovereign over the state, the French Revolution simply replaced one authoritarian system with another. The American Revolution was for individualism. The French Revolution was for collectivism. The French revolution started with high hopes at Versailles and ended twenty-five years later in the bloody fields of Waterloo. The key to understanding how it went so wrong is to understand the concept of "egality."

The word egality is very different from the word equality. Instead of lifting everyone up, or simply treating everyone equal, egalitarianism seeks to beat everyone down to the same level. It seeks to eliminate differences. (With a very large Communist hammer if necessary.)

This doctrine says that it is unfair if someone regularly gets a bigger share of the pie than everyone else, whether they earned it or not. Egalitarianism is not only concerned with economic matters. The general mindset is explained very nicely in the short story, "Harrison Bergeron," by Kurt Vonnegut…

> The year was 2081, and everybody was finally equal. They weren't only equal before God and the law. They were equal every which way. Nobody was smarter than anybody else. Nobody was better looking than anybody else. Nobody was stronger or quicker than anybody else. All this equality was due to the 211th, 212th, and 213th Amendments to the Constitution, and to the unceasing vigilance of agents of the United States Handicapper General.

The "handicapping" worked partly as follows:

> Hazel had a perfectly average intelligence, which meant she couldn't think about anything except in short bursts. And George, while his intelligence was way above normal, had a

> little mental handicap radio in his ear. He was required by law to wear it at all times. It was tuned to a government transmitter. Every twenty minutes or so, the transmitter would send out some sharp noise to keep people like George from taking unfair advantage of their brains.

Science fiction you say? Similar things are happening in the world of business through government regulation all the time.

This perversion of the concept of equality completely obliterates its original meaning and runs roughshod over Liberty. After all, what is "fair?"

Individualists, such as the original Americans, would argue that it is fair that each man keeps the products of his own intelligence, knowledge, efforts, and ability, since each man has a natural and inalienable right to his own life.

A socialist would argue that it is "fair" that each person have an equal share of the "wealth," whether they earned it or not. In practice, this means that those who work and produce will have to give up part of what they produce for those who produce less and may not even work at all. The only way to get from point A to point B is to complete bypass our founding principle of liberty and a man's right to his own life. That is the essence of injustice, not justice.

But socialists are not interested in liberty—that "outmoded" idea is completely incompatible with their "noble" ideals: specifically, that the individual exists to serve society.

And the second problem this idea of equality of outcome brings about is this: who decides what is fair?

As a practical matter, those in power do of course. And from the answer to that question we can see the reason we are in the fix we are in. Once a free people abandons the sanctity of liberty and individual rights, and legalizes the idea of robbing Peter to pay Paul, there is no end to that process.

The leaders, who were supposed to be tasked with safeguarding liberty, protecting property, and providing for the common defense, become usurpers of liberty and violators of property rights! They become little Caesars or Kings, looting from the producers, and then stepping out onto the Royal Balcony to dispense coins to the "favored" groups, the minions that put them in office.

Henry Hazlitt summed up Marxism as follows...

> The whole gospel of Karl Marx can be summed up in a single sentence: Hate the man who is better off than you are. Never under any circumstances admit that his success may be due to his own efforts, to the productive contribution he has made to the whole community. Always attribute his success to the exploitation, the cheating, the more or less open robbery of others. Never under any circumstances admit that your own failure may

> be owing to your own weakness, or that the failure of anyone else may be due to his own defects — his laziness, incompetence, improvidence, or stupidity.

It is almost beyond belief that we are moving toward socialism and Marxism today in America. The economics and morality of it are both laughable. The efficacy of it has been disproved time and time again. Collectivism didn't work for the Pilgrims at Plymouth Rock in 1620, and it hasn't worked anywhere since then either.

The great free market economists have proven this over and over and all the economic statistics bear it out. But we don't even need statistics. All we need to do is open our eyes and look at recent history. Look at the United States vs. Soviet Russia. Look at East Berlin vs. West Berlin. Look at Hong Kong vs. Mao's China. Look at North Korea vs. South Korea, and on and on. Look at the collapse of the socialist welfare states in Greece and Ireland and the UK right now.

And we know what lies at the end of that dead end "egalitarian" road: either the violence of a Nazi Germany or Soviet Russia, the French Reign of Terror, decades of stagnation before the final collapse, or the pathetic destitution of the prison island of Cuba.

It seems that we may have superficially learned the lessons of socialism, but we've never truly learned the principles of Liberty or the moral superiority of capitalism. So we keep drifting in the wrong direction, pulled on a rope by our misguided, corrupt and power-mad politicians.

Socialism's Assault On The Middle Class

The irony is, although socialist politicians play the class warfare game, and rail against "tax cuts for the rich," it is not the "rich" that fill the royal coffers of our "leaders"— it is primarily the middle class.

The fact of the matter is, because of our out-of-control government spending and our unjust tax system, the top 50% of wage earners pay a disproportionate 96% of the taxes. Only a small sliver at the top is truly wealthy. The vast majority of that group is the middle class. This gap is narrowing as we speak. In fact, our current Administration is racking up debts that will be virtually impossible to repay, while narrowing the tax base at the same time (50% of Americans now pay zero income tax).

Writing in "The American" Magazine, Economist Stephen Moore breaks down the numbers from 2007 (it's gotten far worse since then):

> The wealthiest 1 percent of the population earn 19 percent of the income but pay 37 percent of the income tax. The top 10 percent pay 68 percent of the tab. Meanwhile, the bottom 50 percent—those below the median income level—now earn 13 percent of the

income but pay just 3 percent of the taxes. These are proportions of the income tax alone and don't include payroll taxes for Social Security and Medicare.

In other words, the government expects 10% of the population to pay roughly 70% of the tax burden. The wagon is getting heavier and heavier, yet the number of people expected to pull it is getting smaller and smaller. Honest people that are truly concerned about what is "fair," must admit that this is grossly unfair and unsustainable and neither the math, nor the morality of it, adds up.

This "progressive" tax system itself is a holdover from Marx and was in fact one of the 10 points of his Communist Manifesto. It's no coincidence that Marx wanted a heavy tax penalty on those who produced the most ("from each according to his ability, to each according to his needs"), and it's also no coincidence that the American Revolution began with a tax revolt.

Outside of using direct violence, it's primarily through the mechanism of taxation that the government can confiscate our property and control our lives. If you control someone's livelihood (income), you control his life.

The Psychology Of Individualists and Collectivists

Capitalism and socialism are social systems created by different types of people. So to truly understand capitalism and socialism, it's important to understand the way people think. Why are some people staunchly individualist, while others are oriented toward collectivism? At bottom, one of the key differences between an individualist and a collectivist, is a difference in attitudes and general view of the world and of human nature itself.

The stance of the individualist is toward reality. The goal of the individualist is to shape reality to meet his needs. The principle consistent with this view of the word is individual liberty. The human relationship view that is consistent with this attitude is that of a trader, in which free men enter into voluntary exchanges with one another so that each side wins.

They speak of goals and achievements through competition, cooperation and value creation. The social system that is consistent with this view of the world is lasseiz-faire capitalism.

The individualist does not object to living in society with other people. He objects to living in society as a serf or a slave. The Founding Fathers were individualists. The men and women who built this country were individualists.

The individualist believes that men are inherently good and therefore there is no need to brand them with "original sin" or chain their minds or their actions (until and unless they violate the rights of others).

By contrast, the stance of the collectivist is towards other people.

The goal of the collectivist is to use other people to meet his ends. The human relationship view that is consistent with this view of the world is that of master and slave. Exchanges in this view must always be win-lose. They speak of "redistribution," and "service" and "sacrifices."

The social system consistent with this view of the world is Socialism. Kant and Marx were collectivists. Hitler and Stalin were collectivists. Ted Kennedy, Barack Obama, George W. Bush, John McCain, and Hillary Clinton are also collectivists, and by the way, when you hear politicians like them, imbued with the master-servant mentality, speak of "sacrifice" and "service," don't think for a minute that they intend to be the servants.

The difference between an Obama, a Kennedy, a Bush, or a Clinton and a Marx, a Lenin, or a Hitler, is only a matter of degree and tactics, not in basic outlook and philosophy. The anti-freedom ideas espoused by socialists like Hillary Clinton, Barack Obama, Ted Kennedy, George Bush and almost all Democratic and Republican politicians, have consequences when taken to their logical conclusion. Robespierre, Marx, Stalin, Lenin, Mao, Castro, Chavez and Hitler, have already shown us those logical consequences.

The collectivist believes that men are inherently evil and therefore their minds and actions must be chained and controlled through force of the State. This is a remnant of the Christian concept of original sin and the innate depravity of man.

As a thought experiment, pretend for a moment that the United States was divided in half geographically, with individualists on one side and collectivists on the other. Which side do you think would succeed and prosper?

Would it be the individualist side? Where people are pursuing their own goals and dreams, taking responsibility for their own lives, working cooperatively with others by means of voluntary exchange, and respecting the life, liberty, and property of every other person equally and impartially?

Or would it be the collectivist side? Where many people run to government for the fulfillment of their needs... trade their liberty for security.... seek to gain the levers of government to force their "superior" ideas on the "masses"... and seek to "equalize" and "level the playing field" by taking from those who have more and distributing to those who have less?

Which side of the country would have more growth, more business, more jobs, more prosperity? A higher quality of life overall?

We've already made the experiment actually. Just compare the United States of the 19th century to the Soviet Union of the 20th century. Collectivists need individualists because collectivists live parasitically off the production of others. They create nothing of value themselves. That's why they ultimately resort to force by usurping government power. Individualists do not need collectivists and could succeed and prosper quite well without them.

That's why it's so important to understand the philosophy and psychology behind political systems. Ultimately, it comes down to the way people THINK.

At the moment, the collectivist side appears to be winning, so let's dig a little deeper into this unprecedented resurgence of big government in these United States of America....

CHAPTER 5
THE RETURN OF THE IRON HEEL

Out of the decay of self-seeking capitalism, it was held, would arise that flower of the ages, the brotherhood of man.

– From "The Iron Heel", by Jack London

In the early 1900's, many American writers and intellectuals were enthralled with the idea of Socialism. One of them was Jack London.

Now, in interest of full disclosure, I should say that I am a big fan of Jack London's work. And his life was as heroic as his fiction if you know his biography. He lived more in his forty short years than most do in a hundred. He was prolific and authored more than thirty books before the time he died at the age of forty. Although his most famous book was *The Call Of The Wild*, he also wrote many books with social and economic themes.

In fact, in his 1908 book, "The Iron Heel," he prophesied a fascist future in which the strong enslaved the weak… in which purges and secret police terrorized the populace… in which fleeing the country was the only way to escape… in which state organized terror ended in violence… and all of it came true. In 1948, critic Philip Foner wrote that it was "probably the most amazingly prophetic work of the 20th century."

Foner was right, it was prophetic, but there was just one little problem: Jack's prophecies came true under the rule of socialism, not under capitalism as he and his fellow intellectuals had predicted. London and others based their views on a completely false premise about capitalism. Although he was correct in predicting the rise of fascism, he was dead wrong about its cause. He felt that fascism would be the form that capitalism took as it gained political power. But he had it backwards. Fascism is the form socialism takes when the state exerts control over corporations and capital.

It is the state and only the state that controls coercive power, not capitalists or corporations.

Never forget that.

For evidence, we need consult none other than the father of fascism, Benito Mussolini. He wrote this for The Italian Encyclopedia in 1932 on the subject of fascism:

> Fascism conceives of the State as an absolute, in comparison with which all individuals or

> groups are relative, only to be conceived of in their relation to the State. The conception of the Liberal State is not that of a directing force, guiding the play and development, both material and spiritual, of a collective body, but merely a force limited to the function of recording results: on the other hand, the Fascist State is itself conscious and has itself a will and a personality -- thus it may be called the "ethic" State....

The difference between fascism and communism is that, in communism, the state owns everything outright; in fascism, a thin veneer of private ownership is maintained while the state exercises control over industry. As you can see, there is a definite fascist element to our current situation given the American government's control over private corporations in the financial, health care, energy and auto industries. Subsidizing them is a big part of controlling them.

Note also, that Mussolini conceives the role of that state as a "directing force, guiding the play and development, both material and spiritual, of a collective body." Do you see how much that differs from the views of the Founders—and how perfectly it describes the role of the state in our current society?

Despite his brilliance, Jack London was hopelessly, colossally wrong about socialism and where it would lead because he was operating on a false Marxist premise—namely, that the masses who do all of the world's work are being exploited by a minority of "privileged" capitalists by virtue of their control and influence over the government.

Given the context of the times he grew up in, I believe we can forgive Jack London. There is much evidence that in his later years he became disillusioned with socialism. That's no wonder, because his life itself was one of heroic individualism. At the time he became the "boy socialist" of Oakland, CA, he was young and poor and reacting to what he saw around him during a period of his life when he was a laborer. It is difficult to understand and appreciate how a great machine was built when you are looking at it from the perspective of one cog in the machine. He was also influenced by the progressive movement and by ivory tower intellectuals. He had no way of knowing what the results of the socialist "revolution" would be in practice. He would be horrified to know that it was the utopian dreams of the socialists that led to the Iron Heel. He would be shocked to learn that it was capitalism that would lead to the closest approximation humans will ever have of anything resembling a "brotherhood of man."

But now we do know. There are 150 million dead in the 20th century thanks to various forms of socialism.

So can we forgive those who advocate, support, sanction, or turn a blind eye to socialism today?

The Vision Of The Anointed

As evidenced by the history of the past 100 years, collectivists (socialists, fascists, communists, modern day Democrats, and yes, many Republicans) believe that they, through the power of government, can enforce their wishes on other people at the point of a gun (albeit indirectly through legislation) in order to serve "the greater good." They believe that the ends justify the means. Their methods vary in degree but they all share the same world-view and basic premise: that the individual can and should be sacrificed to the group (state, society, country, or religion).

Whereas the Communists had no problem using direct force and violence, our modern day socialists are more into "soft" tyranny (as of yet). They prefer to use the voting booth, lobbying, activism, intimidation and legislation—but they differ only in the means, not the desired ends.

Make no mistake friends, with our current administration, the Iron Heel has come to America. It's been covered in velvet so you can't see it, but it is pressing down hard and it is pressing down fast.

Unlike the Founding Fathers, collectivists believe that a man does not have a right to exist for his own sake, that his life and property do not truly belong to him, but that he exists in order to serve society (just as Mussolini did). In addition to, "From each according to his ability, to each according to his need," Marx also said, "The history of all existing society is the history of class struggle." That may have been true under feudalism, but it is a patently false view when you are talking about a free (capitalist) society; yet it is the still the prism through which his fellow travelers see the world.

There is another element that drives this as well: hubris. Many in the political class believe that they are the anointed, or the "affluent intelligentsia," as Hillary Clinton once put it, who will mold and shape the "masses" according to their own visions (for the "good" of we ignorant masses of course).

As Lenin said, "the masses must be driven to their salvation."

At a Democratic fundraiser for Senator Barbara Boxer in June of 2004, Hillary Clinton said this to the audience about the Bush tax cuts, "Many of you are well enough off that ... the tax cuts may have helped you. We're saying that for America to get back on track, we're probably going to cut that short and not give it to you. We're going to take things away from you on behalf of the common good."

Wow. That's pretty unambiguous, Comrade Clinton.

Or as candidate Obama told "Joe the Plumber," he only wants to raise his taxes so he can "spread the wealth." Karl would be proud of you, Mr. Obama.

And what exactly gives these politicians the right to take property away from some Americans and give it to other Americans for their version of "the common good?"

Democratic and Republican politicians alike are imbued with the Marxian (and false) master-slave mentality. They wrongly believe the choice is to either rule or be ruled, and they of course intend to be the rulers. So they seek power. They gain their power through the tried and true socialist tactic of segmenting society into various "classes," each with allegedly conflicting interests.

They pander politically to these "pressure" groups. They then steal money from some (through enforced taxation), in order to promise handouts in exchange for votes from other groups. The socialist politician has no problem with looting money from ten people if he is confident the proceeds will buy him votes from fifteen people.

"Count the cost that working families are paying while the privileged ride high and reap the rewards," said Senator John Kerry during his failed campaign for the Presidency. This is classic Marxist dogma. It implies that high income earners don't work, but instead have made their money by "exploiting" working families. This, from a man that married into a fortune of more than $500 million, and essentially lives off the wealth created by a great capitalist (the system he likes to rail against). It's not those who have achieved their wealth honestly that "ride high" and reap unjust rewards, Mr. Kerry. The true privileged ones "riding high," are you and your fellow political elites who seek to ride all of us, "booted and spurred."

But we've seen pompous demagogues pretending to be friends of the "working people" countless times before. As the economist and historian Thomas Sowell says…

> Most people who read "The Communist Manifesto" probably have no idea that it was written by a couple of young men who had never worked a day in their lives, and who nevertheless spoke boldly in the name of "the workers." Similar offspring of inherited wealth have repeatedly provided the leadership of radical movements, with similar pretenses of speaking for "the people."

Does anyone with half a brain buy the demagoguery of these politicians anymore?

Contrast the views of Obama, Kerry and Clinton with the Founding Fathers…

> Government is instituted to protect property of every sort; as well that which lies in the various rights of individuals, as that which the term particularly expresses. This being the end of government, that alone is a just government which impartially secures to every man whatever is his own.
> — James Madison

> A wise and frugal government, which shall restrain men from injuring one another, which shall leave them otherwise free to regulate their own pursuits of industry and improvement, and shall not take from the mouth of labor the bread it has earned. This is the sum of good government, and this is necessary to close the circle of our felicity. —

> Democracies have been found incompatible with personal security or the rights of property; and have in general been as short in their lives as they have been violent in their death.
>
> — James Madison

> The moment that idea is admitted into society that property is not as sacred as the Laws of God, and that there is not a force of law and public justice to protect it, anarchy and tyranny commence. Property must be sacred or liberty cannot exist.
>
> — John Adams

> The Natural Rights of the colonists are these: first, a right to life; second, to liberty; third to property; together with the right to support and defend them in the best manner they can.
>
> — Samuel Adams

Again, the purpose of government is to protect liberty and property, not "redistribute" it! Liberty is the end of proper government; it is not the means to some other end.

In reality, America's wealthiest have exploited nobody, quite the contrary. They are the ones that have created prosperity and lifted up the rest of society through their ability, inventions, products, years of work, services, job creation, risk-taking, capital, and long-term efforts.

Most business owners, especially small business owners, work far longer hours and deal with far more stress than their employees. It's the owner or entrepreneur that has everything on the line. He is the one that has responsibility for the entire enterprise. He is the one that will be ruined if it fails and wakes up at 3am with his brain on fire at the thought of it, consumed with all the things he has to do. He is the one who has to deal with the harsh, unyielding realities of profit and loss.

He is the one that has to create something of value to others—and be able to produce it and market it and sell it within the context of intense competitive pressures. And, increasingly these days, now he has to do it while contending with massive new problems created by politicians and government intervention into the economy.

It is not political parasites and posturing politicians that would should admire. It is the businessmen, the risk takers, the innovators, the entrepreneurs, that are the true economic heroes of this country. It is the efforts of the most able, the most intelligent, the hardest working and the most productive members of a free society that create the livelihoods and raise the standard of living for all (all who are willing to work that is).

Nobody said it better than Ayn Rand...

> America's abundance was created not by public sacrifices to "the common good," but by the productive genius of free men who pursued their own personal interests and the making of their own private fortunes. They did not starve the people to pay for America's industrialization. They gave the people better jobs, higher wages and cheaper goods with every new machine they invented, with every scientific discovery or technological advance — and thus the whole country was moving forward and profiting, not suffering, every step of the way.

In a free society, one individual's wealth does not come at the expense of any other individual. The exact opposite is true. If a man has become wealthy in a free society, then he has provided enormous benefits and values to his fellow men.

Socialism is Theft

Capitalism is a system of production and value creation that requires men to deal with each other as traders, exchanging value for value on a mutually voluntary basis. By contrast, the socialist system is a system of expropriation, in which some men seek to obtain values from other men at the point of a gun. That's all it is. It is the economic equivalent of cannibalism.

It is the freedom to pursue our own values, exchange values with others (both material and spiritual), and seek our own happiness here on earth that made America great. America is the last bastion of individualism in the world today. That is why we are hated by collectivists of both religious and secular varieties (Islamists and Socialists-Communists).

It is an absolute crime against our country and a slap in the face to our Founders that we allow politicians to continue to lead us down this socialist road (and we have no one but ourselves to blame).

By the way, this current path of democratic disintegration was entirely predictable and it is something that the Founders were painfully aware of and warned against repeatedly when they formed our Government. As men who valued Liberty above all else, they had an abhorrence for Democracy.

Why? Consider this statement:

> A democracy cannot exist as a permanent form of government. It can exist only until the voters discover that they can vote themselves largesse out of the public treasury. From that moment on, the majority always votes for the candidate promising the most benefits from the public treasury—with the result that democracy always collapses over a loose fiscal policy, always to be followed by dictatorship.

The above was written in the 1600's by an English Professor name Alexander Tyler—and he was writing about the fall of the Athenian Republic some 2000 years prior to that!

There are very few original ideas indeed.

Ben Franklin put it this way, "democracy is two wolves and a lamb voting over what to have for dinner."

This irrational and immoral concept of income redistribution and equality of outcome is one of the key rationalizations behind all of the policies of the welfare state. All welfare states are nothing more than giant Ponzi schemes that will eventually collapse under their own weight. That's what happened to Russia and it's what is happening to Europe as we speak. It is also what will happen to America if we continue on our present course.

Leaving morality and economic efficacy aside for a moment, it's a simple matter of demographics and math. When you have more people taking from a system than paying into it, that system eventually goes bankrupt.

Here is one of the most succinct and lucid explanations I've ever seen of socialism in action. It comes from a book called *Diving the Wealth*, by the late Economist Howard E. Kershner:

> Socialism claims that a higher standard of living can be attained if the state owns or controls the means of production. In order to prove its case, a socialist government has to spend more to do more things for an ever growing numbers of people.
>
> Appropriations for welfare are increased. Money is spent on public housing. Rent subsidies are provided. Social security, Medicare, and Medicaid payments grow larger and larger. Scholarships and pensions are increased, and qualifications for getting them are relaxed. Minimum wage laws are enacted and the rate is increased. Fringe benefits, such as maternity leave are increased. Hours are shortened.
>
> As one group gets something, other groups are unhappy unless they get more. So, group after group. So the socialist politician who promises the most keeps himself in office. He is quite ready to tax ten people and distribute the proceeds to 20 people. Indeed, he will sacrifice ten votes if he is pretty sure of getting 11 or 12 in return. Once we concede to government the power of taking money from some and giving it to others, the process will

> not stop until the last bone of the last taxpayer is picked bare and we are all reduced to something approaching a common denominator. That is to say, under Socialism all except the top bureaucrats, their favorites and essential technicians are headed for the poverty line.

And of course, that is exactly the process that has been played out time and time again in every single country that has adopted socialism. So why on earth do some Americans keep voting for politicians that are clearly socialists!?

Not only is socialism diametrically opposed to the founding principles of this Republic, it's a stupid and immoral idea that has never worked!

That is precisely why the Founders never granted any such powers to the Federal Government to begin with, and they so forcefully emphasized the sanctity of the unalienable rights to life, liberty, and property for each and every individual.

The Resurgence Of Big Government

What do we have for a Government today? A huge, bureaucratic Leviathan that recognizes NO limits whatsoever on its power and its ability to interfere and meddle in all aspects of our lives.

This is the "state despotic" that Tocqueville warned about in Democracy in America. A Federal Government with an annual budget of more than $3.7 trillion, that believes its proper function is to fix every real or imagined social "problem," control the economy through regulation, set interest rates for financial institutions, subsidize failing companies with taxpayer money, pick winners and losers in the private economy, fire the CEO's of private businesses, steal money from the productive and give it to the unproductive, take over the entire medical industry and generally interfere in almost every aspect of the lives of free men and women. Everything is hyper-regulated these days from the amount of water you can have in a flush toilet to how much "trans fats" are allowable in foods.

The State now loots 40-50% of the entire output of the economy each year and we are running an annual deficit of over $1.5 trillion according to the CBO's numbers. We spend over $600 billion per year just on interest payments on the national debt. And yet, many of our fellow Americans shrug their shoulders and say, "at least the President is trying," "they had to do something," and "I'm ok with that."

Our Federal government seizes the earnings of private citizens, distributes it to corporations, and then uses that "gift" as a club to exact obedience, compelling private companies to make concessions or decisions that they would not have otherwise made. This is America?

The original Americans would have been running for their muskets at even the mere hint of this kind of intervention or the taxes that are taken from us (and will have to be taken from our children in the future) to support all this; yet, today's average American taxpayer works for seven months out of the year to support the government on local, state, and national levels without making so much as a peep.

Can you imagine what the reaction of the Founders' generation would have been to the thought of putting the future income of their children up as collateral to obtain loans from foreign countries!? Well, that's exactly what we are doing now, effectively turning future generations into slaves of foreign governments (mainly the Chinese).

In a mere half a century, we have gone from being the world's creditor to becoming the largest debtor nation in the history of the world. The insanity has gotten to the point that we are now borrowing money from the Communist Chinese, then giving the borrowed money to other countries as "foreign aid," paying interest on those loans—and then sending the bill to the next generation.

We are currently working from January until early August on behalf of the State before we begin to make a dime for our own families! To put it another way, we spend at least half our lives working for the Government. And the shocking thing is we do it like obedient serfs not even realizing our own serfdom. From the beginning of the republic up until the FDR era, Federal spending was typically about 3 percent or less of the national income and spending at all levels (federal, state and local), rarely exceeded 12 percent of national income. Today, we are looking at Federal levels of spending exceeding 40 percent of national income and total government spending roughly 60% of national income.

The American Revolution began with a Tax Revolt. The taxation level they were complaining about was about 1%! They knew, however, that it was the principle that mattered, and once a precedent was set in violation of that principle there would be no stopping further encroachments on their Liberty.

> The fierce spirit of Liberty is stronger in the English colonies probably than in any other people on Earth. It happened you know, sir, that the great contests for freedom in this country were from the earliest times chiefly upon the question of Taxing.
>
> — Edmund Burke, addressing the British House of Commons on the eve of the American Revolution in 1775

The issue of taxation is central to America's founding because taxation is the primary mechanism through which the government violates an individual's inalienable rights (the right to life and property). The avoidance of unjust taxation, and thus the upholding of freedom, was one of the key reasons that immigrants came to America in the first place.

As one Irishman wrote back home to Ulster in 1720:

> Tell all the poor folk of ye place that God has opened a door for their deliverance… all that a man works for is his own, and there are no revenue hounds to take it from us here; there is no one to take away yer Corn, yer Potatoes.

How far we've strayed from Jefferson's vision of a free, self-governing people, determining their own destinies, creatively advancing human progress, taking responsibility for their own lives, and enjoying their inalienable natural rights in their homes, their communities, and in their work.

How close we are to Mussolini's vision of living under a state that acts as, "a directing force, guiding the play and development, both material and spiritual, of a collective body"… a place where the state "organizes the nation, but leaves a sufficient margin of liberty to the individual; the latter is deprived of all useless and possibly harmful freedom, but retains what is essential; the deciding power in this question cannot be the individual, but the State alone…."

Wake up Americans!

CHAPTER 6
PRINCIPLES OF A JUST TAX SYSTEM

> *To compel a man to furnish contributions of money for the propagation of opinions which he disbelieves and abhors, is sinful and tyrannical. ... Excessive taxation... will carry reason & reflection to every man's door, and particularly in the hour of election. —*

If you are angry about taxes, you'd be amazed at just how angry your forefathers were. It's no coincidence that the American Revolution began with a tax revolt. The issue of taxation is central to Liberty because it is the primary way the state can violate rights and plunder the property of individuals.

From the time when the British tried to tax us in 1764, to at least 1913, our opposition to taxes led from one tax rebellion to another. Even the Civil War was a tax rebellion in part.

Despite the claim of our current Vice President that it is "patriotic" to pay more in taxes, that's not how the men who founded this country felt. As free men and honest statesmen, they felt that it was slavish to want to pay more in taxes by turning over the fruits of your own labor to the state.

Our Founding Fathers hated taxes with a passion because they realized the power to tax was the power to destroy. Thomas Paine called taxes, "The greedy hand of government thrusting itself into every corner and crevice of industry."

This view of taxation was the prevalent view during our first century. Writing in the Atlantic Magazine in 1878, Brooks Adams, great grandson of John Adams, said the following:

> All taxation is evil, but heavy taxes, indiscriminately levied on everything... are one of the greatest curses that can afflict a people.

Can you imagine a prominent political family from Massachusetts making such a statement today?

Obviously, we need a strong government devoted to the protection of Liberty and that government needs to fund itself for essential functions. The problem we have today is not that the government collects taxes, it's the amount of taxes collected and the amount of spending that is outside its legitimate functions.

Benjamin Franklin said that if any government collected more than

10% of the income of the people in taxes, you were living under Tyranny. During Franklin's time, the total amount of taxes collected was under 5%. However, with the advent of the income tax in 1913, and the subsequent brainwashing of the American public by socialists, by the middle of the 20th century, most Americans acquiesced to tax rates that would have caused armed rebellions in our first hundred years. With more than 50% of the nation's income now being sucked into the black hole of government, we are indeed living under tyranny by Franklin's definition.

The Founding Fathers, and all champions of Liberty through the ages, believed that taxation—over and above that needed to protect individual liberty—was "legalized plunder," a phrase they used repeatedly.

French Economist, Fredric Bastiat, put it this way in his classic book, *The Law* (1850):

This question of legal plunder must be settled once and for all, and there are only three ways to settle it:

1. The few plunder the many.
2. Everybody plunders everybody.
3. Nobody plunders anybody.

We must make our choice between limited plunder, universal plunder, and no plunder. The law can follow only one of these three.

Bastiat left out one more possibility—the many plunder the few. In a country where at least half its citizens do not pay taxes, yet still have the right to vote, this is the situation we are fast-approaching and it's the most dangerous of all. In fact, the recent "Occupy Wall Street" movement is based on this very communistic idea that the many should fleece the top 1% of income earners and simply seize wealth they did not earn (or have the government seize it on their behalf and direct it to toward them). There are your new Bolsheviks, soon to be occupying a town near you, but could somebody throw them a bar of soap?

The Founders hated direct taxation (the income tax) so they did not levy any direct taxes. Through their studies on the history of taxes, as well as the colonists' general experience with taxation in Europe, they knew that once taxes got their foot in the door they would grow and multiply. In general, the colonists saw taxes as the root of all evil in a free society and they were determined not to repeat European mistakes. Unfortunately, that determination was not maintained by future generations of Americans.

We ignore our history and our heritage at our own peril. By acting like sheep who don't mind being fleeced, we are dooming our children and grandchildren to a socialist future. The national debt is now in excess of $16 trillion! George Bush increased it from $5 trillion to $9 trillion in his eight years in office and Barack Obama has already increased it another $7 trillion in just three short years. But that's only the tip of the iceberg, because that does not include Social Security and Medicare. Most economists put the unfunded liabilities for Social Security and Medicare at $100 trillion.

$100 trillion of debt. Think about that. That is the legacy that the past two generations of Americans will be leaving to their offspring.

Despite these astounding numbers, our current President is still pressing forward with vast spending programs. The current year's budget is over $3 trillion dollars and will cause a deficit of at least $1.4 trillion according the Congressional Budget Office. Mr. Obama also continues to pursue the socialization of the health care and energy industries, which will cost enormous sums of money while strangling those industries and raising the cost of energy and health care for all Americans (while reducing the quality).

In other words, we are on a path to bankrupting this nation.

This is why it's so important to understand the moral principles involved in supporting Liberty and all of the elements that undermine Liberty, including taxation and a government that has gone completely off the rails.

Principles For a Just Tax Code

In his later years, after serving as President and then reflecting on the difficult problem of taxation, Jefferson tried to lay out a just tax philosophy. In an 1816 treatise called "Prospectus on Political Economy," he offered the following ideas…

> 1. A tax should be so framed as to reach every member of Society, and to draw from him equal proportion of the public contribution; and if this be correctly obtained, it is perfection of the function of taxation.
>
> 2. It is the most sacred of the duties of a government to do equal and impartial justice to all it citizens.
>
> 3. To take from one, because it is though that his own industry and that of his fathers has acquired too much, in order to spare others, who, or whose fathers have not exercised equal industry and skill, is to violate arbitrarily the first principle of association, the guarantee to everyone of a free exercise of his industry, and the fruits acquired by it… extra taxation violates it [a law of nature].

In America, we shouldn't even have a tax on income to begin with, let alone a "graduated" or progressive income tax. The idea of the graduated income tax was Karl Marx's. It's a holdover from his Communist Manifesto. Already, most Americans have to work until August of each year before we have one dime to call our own.

Don't believe me? Add up all of the taxes: federal, social security, state, local, excise, property, sales, etc. And yes, social security is a tax of 15% on everyone. The fact that the employer pays half just means that employees get 7.5% less than they would have received in salary. So it's the employee that pays the 15%, just like a self-employed person. Then add in the higher costs of everything due to government regulations and mandates.

Also, be sure not to forget inflation, which is the cruelest tax of all, because it affects everybody, even the truly poor. Every time the government engages in money printing, or "quantitative easing," inflation is sure to rise in the future and every dollar in your pocket will buy less and less.

The government taxes virtually every aspect of our lives... there is the federal income tax, social security tax, Medicare tax, federal unemployment tax, state unemployment tax, corporate income tax, gift tax, gasoline tax, tobacco tax, property tax, state income tax, sales tax, car excise tax, boat tax, hotel room tax, alternative minimum tax, luxury taxes, capital gains taxes, tariffs, worker's compensation tax, and many more... then, when we die we are taxed once more for good measure with the estate tax (on money that has already been taxed!).

Every year, the Americans for Tax Reform Foundation and the Center for Fiscal Accountability calculate Cost of Government Day. This is the day on which the average American has earned enough gross income to pay off his or her share of the spending and regulatory burdens imposed by government at the federal, state, and local levels.

In 2011, Cost of Government Day falls on August 12. Working people worked 224 days out of the year just to meet all costs imposed by government—a full 26 days longer than the previous year. In other words, in 2011 the cost of government consumed 61.34 percent of national income. In their report, ATR writes, "Americans have lost 29 days of the calendar year thanks to Obama's overspending and regulatory zeal. 2011 marks the third straight year COGD has fallen in August. Prior to the Obama Administration, COGD had never fallen later than July 21."

Do we want our children to have to work until August of every year before they have a dime to call their own? Do we really want to leave them with a debt burden of more than $100 trillion hanging over their heads like the sword of Damocles? If our current Administration is allowed to continue these big government socialist programs, our children and grandchildren will be working as serfs of the state until probably September or October of each year! At what point do we call it slavery?

We are still paying for the massive entitlement programs FDR pushed through such as Social Security. Social Security is a giant Ponzi scheme that now has a $50 trillion unfunded liability that by itself could bankrupt the country once the baby boomers start collecting in 2012. It was flawed, unconstitutional and immoral from the beginning and should never have been enacted in America. Everyone would have been far better off if they had been allowed to keep all of the money that was taken from them via the social security payroll tax.

Once upon a time in America, the hard working, frugal, and industrious could get ahead because they could keep 90% of what they were able to earn. If they saved, made smart investments, and built their capital they could even get rich or achieve financial independence. There was also a gold standard to ensure that a dollar was actually worth a dollar. It was very possible to live comfortably off one income so mothers could stay home and raise their children if they chose to do so. Today, that is virtually impossible in most parts of the country. Two income households have become the norm.... You need one income to take care of your family and the other income to take care of your taxes!

Some people like to rationalize all of this, particularly when it comes to our current President's plans. He says he will only raise taxes on high income earners. To that, some say, "if you have to pay more in taxes because you're making over $200K, that's a good problem to have."

No, being stolen from is not a good problem to have. But even more importantly, thinking it's ok to take more from someone that happens to have more money than you is not a good principle to have. And to go along with something like that is the height of hypocrisy.

To get to that level of earnings, most people have to go through years of work and struggle. By what right does Federal Government come in and take 40% of the money those individuals earn when other individuals pay 15% or nothing at all? The entire system is immoral and unfair.

Think about this: let's pretend we have a flat tax of 15% and person A makes $50,000. He pays $7,500 in taxes. Person B makes $500,000, so he pays $75,000 in taxes, or 10X as much as A.

Does person B use more public services than person A? No, most likely, he uses less. So why exactly should he pay 10X as much as person A? Even that is unfair on its face but certainly nobody could logically argue that Person B is not paying his "fair share." He is paying 10X more than person A while using fewer public services!

Now please tell me why the person making $500,000 should pay a higher percentage on his income when he's already paying far more, even with our fictional flat tax rate?

President Obama wants to raise the Federal rate to an obscene 39%. (At one point, FDR raised it up to 90%). So under Mr. Obama's plan, person B in our example would pay well over $150,000 in taxes vs. just $7,500 for person B.

Please tell me how that's "fair?" By what logic?

And how will those who don't mind the "soak the rich" strategy feel when they reach that level? "Do not dig a hole for somebody else, lest you fall in it yourself."

And of course, those who believe Mr. Obama's pledge about only raising taxes on the "rich" probably believe in the tooth fairy too.

Taxes and Stupid Marxist Lies

Socialists try to justify all of this theft by implying the so-called rich got their money at the expense of someone else or "on the backs of the little guy." That's stupid Marxist lie #1. It comes from his "exploitation" theory of labor as we discussed.

Socialists say they just want to "spread the wealth around." I don't know about you, but I want other people to succeed. I don't envy their success. I don't want the government to take money from them and give it to me. Likewise, I don't expect the money I've earned to be taken from me and given to others either.

In the example above, did person B steal his money to make that income? No, he earned it because he works harder, smarter, or has skills that are more valuable to others that they willingly pay him for. Many people in those income brackets are small business owners and entrepreneurs who risk their own capital, work six or seven days a week, and spend years building a business. Others are people like Doctors, Dentists and other professionals that have specialized skills and often work very long hours. People like those are the ones who provide jobs for others, not to mention the products and services that we all need in our daily lives.

If anything, the government should be sending gifts to those high income earners with big “THANK YOU" notes and flowers attached, to thank them for paying so much more than anyone else in taxes and also providing products, services, and livelihoods for others.

Think about a typical small business owner for example. Struck with an idea for doing something better, or simply by the desire to “be his own boss,” he starts a new fledgling businesses while already working full time. So he is already paying a "fair share" of taxes. He then works the equivalent of two full-time jobs, risks his own money, recruits investors, builds the business, deals with countless obstacles and hurdles, takes on debt, almost goes bust, and eventually makes it successful. (Of course, we are talking about a rare exception here, because, although almost all of those who start new businesses go through the above, they usually end up going bust. More than 95% of all small businesses started fail within the first five years.)

To stay with our example, let’s say the service started by this entrepreneur is a B2B service that saves other companies money, so it's a net value to society. After spending years building the business, the company eventually succeeds and provides livelihoods for thirty employees. The government did absolutely NOTHING to help him build that business and he did not take one penny that belonged to anybody else along the way.

So tell me again why “society” has the right to loot far more from him percentage-wise than the person making $50,000 working at the post office, who never worked more than 40 hours in his life?

"Because he has it," is not a valid answer. That's like saying it's ok for a thief to rob a bank, but not a convenience store, simply because the bank has more money than the convenience store. Those who say we should tax the rich more simply because “they have it” have the morals of a bank robber.

This idea of “progressive taxation” is socialism once again. It is based on envy and thievery. That’s why Marx was so adamant about it being the inevitable “evolution” after the capitalist stage. He knew that socialism could never create wealth on its own… he needed freedom and capitalism to actually create the goods, services, and wealth of society first… Then once it was “ripe,” the socialists would take over and control the means of production.

Like all socialists, our current politicians love to vilify the rich by implying they are not paying their "fair share," so we must raise their taxes even further. “Businessmen are evil and corporations get rich through exploitation" is stupid Marxist lie #2.

Now, some may say, "but the government needs money to operate and provide services." Yes it does. But the question is: what services does the government in a free country need to provide? America is based on a Constitution and Bill of Rights that clearly defines what the Federal government is supposed to do. It can be summed up in three words: Protect Individual Liberty.

There are three essential functions needed to protect Liberty:

1. A criminal justice system.
2. A volunteer military to defend the nation from foreign invaders.
3. A system of civil courts to enforce contracts and arbitrate disputes.

These are three indispensable services as well as monumentally difficult tasks. We all know that we owe our security to the heroic efforts of the police on a local level and the armed forces at the national level. Often overlooked is the critically important day-to-day work of the civil court system.

A civil court system provides a legally binding forum in which the millions of disputes each year between honest men can be settled peacefully. In a way, this may be the most important function a government can provide, because criminals are a small minority while contractual protection is a daily necessity for the millions of transactions that happen every day in our economy and keep the system running.

Now, if the State was limited to those three functions, how much would it need to collect in taxes? It's difficult to say currently, because so much of the Federal budget is comprised of items outside these proper functions. Social Security and Medicare alone account for more than one-third of the current $3.8 trillion budget, while defense amounts to 16% of the budget. If the government was limited to the above three functions, it's certainly reasonable to expect that the federal income tax burden on American households would drop by 80%. Don't hold your breath waiting for that to happen however.

Choking The Golden Goose

The immorality of socialism is not the only problem. The other problem is what these "soak the rich" policies do to the economy and the country overall. Every child knows the fable of the goose and the golden eggs. The people that start, manage and invest in businesses are the geese in our society. The higher income earners are the most productive people in society. Placing burdensome taxes on them is the equivalent of choking the geese that lay the golden eggs we all need.

The first thing that happens when you choke them is they slow down their production. Why work extra hard and poke your head above the $200K line when 40% of it will be stolen from you by the Federal government alone?

The second thing it does is slows down investment. Why would you risk your capital in the middle of an economy that is in the midst of a downward spiral caused by a foolish and rapacious government? How can you make any rational long term investments in any industry when the government can come in and change the rules of the game on a whim? How can you be confident of a return on your investment when the government is using taxpayer money to fund competitors in industries that politicians and the liberal elite favor (Solyndra for but one example).

Marxist taxation and regulatory environments like ours provide a dis-incentive to production and investment. Increasing taxes on businesses will also force businesses to raise prices on goods and services. In some markets that's not possible due to competition. So they will have to try to cut expenses, which usually means laying off workers. As a result of all this, what happens? The economy doesn't grow, it declines. Unemployment rises. Prices rise also. And the net result for the government is it collects LESS tax revenue because of the economic stagnation. This is not news, this is all Economics 101.

The way to increase employment and achieve economic growth is to do the opposite of what our current administration is doing. Provide incentives to the most productive people by lowering their marginal taxes. Lower or eliminate the taxes on businesses. Eliminate the capital gains tax to encourage investment. This has all been proven time and time again in this and many other countries.

What Reagan and Kennedy Agreed On

For example, Census Bureau statistics bear out the benefits of President Reagan's 25% across-the-board tax cuts in the early 1980's. Americans prospered and their lives improved with lower inflation (from 13.5% in 1980 to 4.1% in 1988); lower interest rates (from 18% on a 30 year fixed mortgage in 1981 to 8% in 1987); and outstanding job growth (unemployment had peaked at near 10% in the recession of 1981-1982 and dropped to 5.5% in 1989 once the whole 25% tax cut took effect). The American people kept more of what they earned, saw investments increased, and in the process, enjoyed the creation of 17 million new jobs.

The other side of the coin is that when you raise taxes you ultimately reduce tax revenues, so the government winds up collecting less money — money that's needed for national defense, paying down the debt, etc.

Take the example of the Kennedy tax cuts. President Hoover dramatically increased tax rates in the 1930s and FDR compounded the damage by raising marginal tax rates to more than 90 percent. These high rates persisted through the 50's. Recognizing that such high tax rates were hurting the economy, President Kennedy proposed across-the-board tax rate reductions in 1960. What happened? Tax revenues climbed from $94 billion in 1961 to $153 billion in 1968, an increase of 62 percent (33 percent after adjusting for inflation). Kennedy said the following:

Our true choice is not between tax reduction, on the one hand, and the avoidance of large Federal deficits on the other. It is increasingly clear that no matter what party is in power, so long as our national security needs keep rising, an economy hampered by restrictive tax rates will never produce enough revenues to balance our budget just as it will never produce enough jobs or enough profits... In short, it is a paradoxical truth that tax rates are too high today and tax revenues are too low and the soundest way to raise the revenues in the long run is to cut the rates now.

It seems that if Kennedy were around today, he might be classified as "right wing extremist" by the Department of Homeland Security. Granted, he was no champion of Liberty and his primary motivation in cutting taxes was raising revenues for the Federal Government, not upholding liberty or our Founding principles. However, the example illustrates that the idea that excessive taxes can somehow stimulate economic growth and/or result in more tax revenues is nonsense.

But you see, economic growth is not really the goal of our current crop of socialists—their goal is power and control. First control, then command. Socialists want to "soak the rich" out of their warped idea of fairness. They act as if the government gave the money to those high income earners and now they're the Robin Hoods giving those ill-gotten gains back to the "working people."

But let's remember that Robin Hood was a thief and this idea applied to honest business is childish nonsense. The higher income earners did earn their money and they usually work far longer hours than the "working people." Robin Hood also had a lot less overhead than the government.

To compound the problem, very little of the wealth that is confiscated actually makes it through to the intended recipients. Most of it gets trapped and wasted in the giant web of Washington bureaucracy. To the extent that it does make it to the recipients, it breeds dependence and becomes a vicious cycle that feeds on itself. It chains people to the state and becomes a trap, not a ladder.

The government says they are only taking from the rich, but they are actually taking from both rich and poor at the same time. Confiscatory taxes on high income earners hurt the poor far more than they do the rich. Why? The rich lay people off. They stop spending. They stop creating businesses and providing jobs. Some close their businesses. They stop donating so much to charity.

The ironic thing is that the truly wealthy don't even pay much income tax. The truly wealthy are the Ted Kennedy's, John Kerry's, and George W. Bush's of the world, living off of trust funds that someone else earned for them. The only taxes they pay are on capital gains, which is at a lower rate than the income tax. This is yet another reason why the income tax should be abolished.

But the bottom line is this: theft is theft and there is simply no justification for it.

How A Fair Tax System Would Work

Even under the current framework, there are simple improvements that could be made. As the Founding Fathers recommended, all taxes should be uniform, meaning everyone pays the same percentage rate.

Start with a flat tax across the board of 15% to the federal government. Everyone that has an income must pay it. Once you hit a certain level, let's say $100,000, you pay no more income tax above that level. The government sends you a "thank you" letter for being so productive and paying so much more in taxes than most other people, even though you don't consume more public services.

Now, think about two things: (1) how simple and fair that is. You do not need an Accountant or a 60,000 page tax code; and (2) think about what an incentive that is for hard work and production. If every American knew they could keep 85% of what they earned… and then, if they hit a certain level of earnings, they could keep everything they earned beyond that level, everyone would be working their behinds off to get to that level.

How much better would your life be if you were able to keep 80 or 90%

of everything you earned rather than 40-50%? That is a huge difference that would allow room for savings and investment. You would really be able to build wealth over the long haul. People could become truly financially independent, not beholden to the government or a slave of their creditors like mortgage companies, credit card companies, etc. Relying on something like Social Security in old age would be a non-issue.

It would also result in a virtuous cycle, in which savings and investment increased while more and more money went into the productive sector of the economy spurring further and further economic growth. That's how things were at one time in this country. Before the income tax, entrepreneurs such as Henry Ford could plow all of their profits right back into their business to expand and grow faster.

Alas, we can never get to a world like that if we keep playing around the edges and accepting things as they are. There are various proposals all floating about but they will not work until the American people start demanding that the government beast be put back in its cage and spending is allocated only to the three functions discussed earlier—the military, the courts, and on a local level, the police and related services.

Whether it's done as a flat tax or consumption tax is not really the issue. The question of how to fund the government in a free society is a technical one that can easily be figured out. The main issue is not the how, it's the what.

In order to even get to a place where we can have a discussion about how, we have an ideological battle to fight. In order to fight it properly we need to first understand how we got here—and then there are still many myths to debunk and dragons yet to slay…

CHAPTER 7

HOW AMERICA LOST HER COMPASS

The natural progress of things is for liberty to yield and for government to gain. —

The period from 1876 (when the civil war ended the injustice of slavery) through 1913 (when the Federal Income Tax was enacted) represented the one and only time in history when there was a brief period of freedom in any country in the world.

Sadly, it was not to last.

After the turn of the twentieth century, America began to turn her face away from liberty and tyranny began to reassert itself, just as Jefferson warned it would.

We need to stop fooling ourselves. We are no longer a free country. We no longer have anything remotely resembling what the Founders would call Liberty.

Can Liberty and freedom ever be restored? Not if we don't understand what happened, so let's take a closer look at the history of the major statist encroachments…

Crack #1 In The Liberty Bell – The Progressive Movement

The America conceived by the Founding Fathers lasted little more than a century. The death knell began as the "progressives," inspired by the collectivist ideas of German and French thinkers, began to have great influence in the early 1900's. Unfortunately, there was a significant importation of German philosophy during the period after the Civil War.

Taking their cues from German philosophers such as Kant and Hegel, they began to assert that the American system, with its emphasis on individual liberty and economic laissez faire, was fundamentally wrong—immoral even. They envisioned a better America, based on "fairness" and run by an "elite," who would make decisions for the "ignorant masses." American Progressives thought that the natural rights principles of the Constitution represented the greatest obstacle to political "progress" and "evolution." They were not willing to hold any truths as self-evident.

In fact, the progressives sought to replace the Constitution with a powerful state whose purpose would be the quest of evolutionary "progress" and whose powers would therefore be unlimited.

After all, they would only use their power for good, right?

The novelist William Dean Howells even came up with a name for this Utopian vision in his 1894 novel, "A Traveler From Altruria." Altruria would be the new land of altruism. (As an interesting side note, a commune called Altruria was setup in Sonoma County in 1894 to demonstrate this utopian vision. It went bankrupt after a few months. That should have been an early warning sign but the progressives took no heed.)

The term "progressive" is one of those Orwellian terms that really means the opposite of what it implies. The term "progressive" was (and still is) simply a euphemism for collectivist. What they were trying to make "progress" from, was the ideal of Liberty. What progressives want to do in fact is REGRESS back to the age-old ways of organizing society based on authoritarian rule and primitive tribalism. So, in the Orwellian world we live in, when you hear progressive, think "regressive socialist," or "primitive tribalist," and you will know the truth.

That goes double for today's progressives by the way. It remains one of the most grotesque ironies that progressives are able to put over on the public the idea that they are concerned with progress… that they are the ones who are modern and advanced… that they are the ones concerned with humanity… when the reality is, under that mask, they stand for nothing more than the backwardness of tribal rule by force and intimidation. What they are interested in doing primarily is using the power of government to force their opinions and ideas on others. All too often, those ideas include the notion that the government should siphon money from those who earned it and give it to them.

Again, socialists are wonderful at manipulating the language for their purposes. They also co-opted the term "liberal." In the classical tradition, a Liberal was someone who wanted to "liberate" man from the authoritarian rule of the Church and the King. It was someone who advocated the Enlightenment values of reason, individual liberty, scientific pursuit, and human progress. As a result, classical liberals stood for Liberty in all human spheres — intellectual, moral and economic. They were for free minds, free people and free markets. Needless to say, modern liberals are for none of the above. They want state control of markets as well as state control of speech and media via government regulations such as the Fairness Doctrine and Net Neutrality (more Orwellian terms), and through the soft tyranny of "political correctness."

Let The Regulation Begin

The first shot across the bow from the progressives was the 1887 Interstate Commerce Commission Act, which established the first Federal Regulatory body, designed to supervise railroad rates. This set the precedent and led to the Sherman Antitrust Act of 1890. It gave sweeping powers to the federal authorities to punish a newly concocted "economic crime" in vague, undefined language (called "restraint of trade").

It was a landmark because it represented the beginning of government control and regulation of the economy in America. It was passed by a Republican Congress who thought they were appeasing the reformers and never thought it would actually be used or enforced. Were they ever wrong.

As Dr. Leonard Peikoff points out in his book, *The Ominous Parallels: The End Of Freedom In America*, this is the pattern that has played out time after time since then, as liberty has receded and tyranny has advanced…

The factors involved in the early regulatory acts indicate the pattern operative in all the turning points of the subsequent decades. Insistent, philosophically generated pressure from the left inaugurates each new development. Popular confusion permits the anti-statist nation of the Enlightenment to accept new increments of state power, one at a time, without any idea of the trend's intellectual sources or meaning. Conservative default, moral and political, leaves the public permanently disarmed.

The Progressive Movement of the early 1900's in America, consisted mainly of men who had been educated in the German collectivist theories of the late 1800's. This was the first generation of Americans who had been trained in this fashion. Prior to that, education had always been in the classical tradition, emphasizing the Enlightenment values of reason, liberty, individualism, and self-reliance.

The Progressive's believed—like all power-lusters before or since—that the power of the state held the solution to most of mankind's problems. Therefore, they would need to control the machinery of government in order to impose their "noble" vision on America.

President Theodore Roosevelt, a dupe of the Progressives, railed against businesses as "malefactors of great wealth." In fact, his faction split from the Republican Party and he ran on the Progressive party ticket in 1912. He became famous for trust-busting and going after "monopolies." Due to his fascinating life and personal charisma, Roosevelt is looked upon favorably by most historians. But the facts are much different than the myth. See Jim

Powell's book, *Bully Boy*, to get the true story on Roosevelt.

As is the case with the "Robber Barons" smear of business tycoons (they were neither robbers nor barons), this "trust busting" and anti-business frenzy was driven by socialist propaganda.

Despite the nonsense about "malefactors of great wealth," the businessmen and entrepreneurs of the late 19th century were quite possibly the greatest force for good that humanity has ever seen. They were creating, inventing and advancing human progress at a pace never seen before or since. Through the investments they made and the industries they built, they were constantly lowering prices of goods and services and bringing vital products and services to the masses at prices they could afford.

For example, despite Roosevelt's whining about Robber Barons, the average price of steel rails fell from $68 to $32 before Roosevelt became president. Thanks to the introduction of new technology, the amount of steel produced in the United States went from 77,000 tons in 1870 to over 10 million tons in 1900. Most of it was produced by a company started by a Scottish immigrant named Andrew Carnegie.

John Rockefeller's Standard Oil, the most hated of the supposed "monopolies," had many competitors and its oil prices were not only lower than those of most of its competitors, they had been falling consistently over the years. It was much the same story in other industries labeled as "monopolies."

Tragically, even some of the great businessmen themselves, such as Andrew Carnegie, got into the progressive's act, which meant they were empowering their own destroyers. Carnegie once said the rich man should give away his "surplus revenues" so as to "produce the most beneficial results for the community—the man of wealth thus becoming the agent and trustee of his poorer brethren." Carnegie even said, "The man who dies thus rich dies disgraced."

But why is it a "disgrace" to die with money in the bank that you have earned honestly? Why is it a "disgrace" to spend it on yourself or your family — or to leave it to your children? Altruists, and apparently Carnegie was one, believe that people have a duty to sacrifice themselves for others. But if so, what happened to the individual's "inalienable right to life, liberty and the pursuit of happiness?" What happened to honoring productive achievement?

That is what happens when businessmen ignore the power of ideas and let so-called intellectuals do their thinking for them. Carnegie guzzled the socialist-altruist Kool-aid as well as that of Christianity. The question here is not whether or not charity is a good thing, it certainly can be as long as it is given freely, the question is whether people of high achievement and great wealth are moral if they don't give away what they have achieved and earned through their own efforts.

Isn't everything that goes into building, creating and achieving that wealth in the first place a much greater moral achievement than the mere act of writing a check to give it away?

This phenomenon of businessmen aiding and abetting their enemies is what Ayn Rand called "the sanction of the victim." We can still see it today with the spectacle of Bill Gates, the world's richest man, calling for "creative capitalism" (which is nothing more than a euphemism for a mix of freedom plus socialist controls and redistribution) and giving away his immense fortune as penance for the sin of being a productive genius who earned great wealth. Or take the doddering Warren Buffet, who apparently has sucked so much money out of the Capitalist system it's addled his brain, claiming that it's fine to tax the rich at far higher rates merely because "they have it." Marx and Lenin would have loved such an eminently useful "capitalist."

This all started with the progressives. Taking their cue from Marx, novelists such as Theodore Dreiser and Frank Norris declared that man was a helpless product of his environment, who would be exploited by capitalists and doomed to poverty and despair—unless he was "helped" by the government.

Sound familiar?

The Educators Grease The Skids

The Progressive movement was not limited to political and economic matters. Thanks to 19th century educators, such as Horace Mann and John Dewey, the fathers of modern education in America, progressives began to develop educational strategies designed to "socialize" the child. This did not mean teaching them to make friends and get along with others. It meant to discourage independent thinking in favor of the consensus thinking of the group. Or to put it another way—to surrender one's mind to the judgment of others.

As Dewey put it…

> The mere absorbing of facts and truths is so exclusively individual an affair that it tends very naturally to pass into selfishness. There is no obvious social motive for the acquirement of mere learning, there is no clear social gain in success thereat.

In other words, he is saying “do not eat the fruit from the tree of knowledge. Do not think for yourself. Because if you do, you will be harder for us to control and shape to our liking.”

This explains why standards in education have plummeted over the years, why Progressive teaching methods consist primarily of class discussions where everyone's opinion is considered equally valid—and why Johnny and Susie can't read, write, add or think. When you throw out logic and independent thinking, you undermine reason, rationality, and truth. Eventually you wind up with a nation that worships at the altar of irrationalism and socialism (“we can’t really be certain about anything… what does the group think?”). Those chickens are coming home to roost today in a variety of ways: from blind faith in politicians… to blind faith in claims of global warming… to blind faith in claims of the supernatural.

The public school movement of the 19th century was the first effort that succeeded in using government power to try to “socially engineer” the people of the United States. This opened a huge new avenue for government intervention into our personal lives on a day to day level.

In the mid 19th century Horace Mann sought to completely replace private schools with the common or public schools. It was the goal of Mann and many other zealous government school advocates to completely abolish the predominate private schools of the time. Horace Mann wrote, "Let the common school be expanded to its capabilities, let it be worked with the efficiency of which it is susceptible, and nine-tenths of the crimes in the penal code would become obsolete; the long catalogue of human ills would be abridged; men would walk more safely by day..."

Again, we can see the utopian socialist mindset at work: If only the government would force everyone into common schools run by the government, crime would disappear and enlightenment would reign.

Horace Mann was dead wrong of course. We would be far better off had education remained private and competitive. Compulsory state education has always been a useful tactic for tyranny as exemplified by communist and socialist regimes throughout the world. As far as the crime rate in the United States, contrary to what Mann thought, it has skyrocketed since the time of compulsory education. It’s also important to note that there is no amendment to the Constitution guaranteeing the "right" to publicly-funded education.

The educators teed up the ball and then the politicians took over.

Picking up where Theodore Roosevelt left off, Woodrow Wilson advanced the progressive cause and its theory of the proper role of government. Before becoming President, Wilson had been president of Princeton and of the American Political Science Association. He has the distinction of being the first Chief Executive to openly criticize the Constitution, once comparing it to "political witchcraft." He was so hostile to Liberty and the self-evident truths of the founding, that he said this during a speech in 1911: "if you want to understand the real Declaration of Independence, do not repeat the preface."

Wilson also deserves credit for the oft-repeated idea that the Constitution is a "living" or "evolving" document. He wrote the following in 1908, "Government is not a machine, but a living thing. It falls, not under the theory of the universe, but under the theory of organic life. It is accountable to Darwin." I guess we could call that the Social Darwinism theory of government: "every government for itself, and to hell with the individual!"

Wilson insisted that the Constitution did not contain any theories or principles, and said that it has "a natural evolution," and can be "one thing in one age, another in another." He wrote that "living political constitutions must be Darwinian in structure and practice."

Wilson's interpretation still dogs us today of course. Barack Obama parroted this dreck in a radio interview back in a 2001 on Chicago Public Radio (WBEZ), saying that it was too bad the Constitution "didn't break free from the limitations placed on it by the Founding Fathers." He lamented that it did not give the Federal government dictatorial powers to "redistribute wealth," and that it focused only on "negative" rights.

The "negative" rights charge is another example of socialist spin. In fact, the Constitution seeks to enforce the positive right of individual liberty… and therefore requires only the negative obligation of leaving others alone by not stealing their property or interfering with their liberty of action. By "positive" rights, statists like Mr. Obama mean that the government should be able to provide for the "needs" of people by seizing the property of Peter and giving it to Paul.

The legacy of the Progressive movement has been unparalleled intervention by government. Labor laws were mandated specifying working conditions and maximum hours. Workmen's compensation was mandated. Businessmen were prosecuted using the Sherman Act. The Clayton Act forbid "unfair" competition. The FTC was established. The Federal Reserve was created to monopolize banking. And then, in 1913, we of course got the

Income Tax, which was the death knell for freedom.

The result was a huge civil service of bureaucrats all working toward the goal of "remaking" America in the image of Bismarck's Germany.

Crack #2: Roosevelt and The "New Deal"

The Progressives set the agenda prior to World War I. But after the war, reeling from the realization that the entire bloody slaughter was senseless, most Americans sought a "return to normalcy." That took the form of the go-go years of the Roaring 20's. But that normalcy was short-lived, because the seeds of destruction had already been sown. In 1929, what would have been a normal economic cycle and short-lived recession, turned out to be a decade long depression thanks to continued government intervention.

Although Wilson and Hoover can take some of the blame, the man that put the "great" into the Great Depression, was Franklin Delano Roosevelt. Contrary to the status he has attained since World War II, FDR was not a hero who "got us out" of the Great Depression. His New Deal undermined the foundations of this country so deeply, we have still not recovered (in fact, it's an open question if we'll ever recover).

One of the most pervasive myths of the last one hundred years is the lie that FDR's New Deal was the cure for the Great Depression. Nothing could be further from the truth. As a matter of fact, FDR and his band of interventionists extended and prolonged the depression. In fact, you could say that they in fact turned a much-needed stock market correction and recession into a Depression.

Understanding what FDR did is crucially important today since our new President is so un-educated or misinformed about economics that he seems to think FDR "saved the economy," and therefore seems hell-bent on repeating FDR's disaster.

Many economists saw what Roosevelt was doing and vehemently opposed him at the time. One was Howard E. Kershner. In his 1936 book, *The Menace of Roosevelt and His Policies*, Kershner pointed out that "under the leadership of President Roosevelt America has smoked economic opium, with resulting dreams and delusions of prosperity through planning and paternalism."

He concluded his analysis by summarizing the points below. As you read them, just substitute "Roosevelt" with "Obama," and you'll get the drift...

> At best, government has always involved a good deal of political racketeering. It was the first and biggest racket ever devised by man, and the fact that it is sometimes carried on by catch words, slogans and the jargon of the so-called economists, instead of swords, guillotines and guns does not make it any less of a racket. How men have struggled, schemed and fought for control of the public purse! How they have used public position and power for private ends!
>
> Mr. Roosevelt ... took charge of our government when it was comparatively simple, and for the most part confined to the essential functions of government, and transformed it into a highly complex, bun-gling agency for throttling business and bedeviling the private lives of free people. It is no exaggeration to say that he took the government when it was a small racket and made a large racket out of it....
>
> In taking the position that the Federal Government in Washington is responsible for the economic condition of the individual, and in putting a vast army of people on federal relief, many of whom now seem to think that government owes them a living, Mr. Roosevelt has sowed to the wind and will reap the whirlwind....
>
> If we are to preserve democracy we must go back to economic freedom. By his persistent advocacy of "socialistic" experiments, his extravagant waste of money, his reckless expansion of public credit, his policy of inflation and tinkering with the currency, his bureaucracy, his catering to class hatreds, his repudiation of promises and loss of faith in government, which his policies have caused — by all this and more, Mr. Roosevelt has endangered our entire heritage of political and economic freedom. Such is the menace of Roosevelt and his policies.

The New Deal picked up where the Progressives left off and turned the country into a giant Welfare State. It was a total repudiation of the laissez-faire capitalism that gave rise to the success of America in her first century.

Like Obama, Roosevelt loved to name "czars." Roosevelt's economic "czars" had two main sources of their ideas—Benito Mussolini and Joseph Stalin. Mussolini favored fascism, while Stalin preferred socialism, but they were essentially two sides of the same rotten coin. Where socialism has the ultimate goal of the state fully taking over the means of production, fascism allowed for nominal private ownership but with full state control.

During the 1930's, American leftists and intellectuals were enamored with the fascist Italy and Soviet Russia. Many of them traveled there to pay homage to Mussolini and Stalin. (FDR was so taken with Stalin he called him "Uncle Joe.") Lenin had referred to these admiring Soviet sympathizers as "useful idiots." Many of these useful idiots wound up as advisors to FDR, and even members of his administration (such as the Communist, Henry Wallace).

Now, was "Uncle Joe" all that bad? After all, in his 4th Inaugural Address, when speaking of the Soviet Union, Franklin Roosevelt said "in order to make a friend, one must be a friend." Roosevelt's friend "Uncle Joe" went on to murder 20 million of his own citizens.

What statists and collectivists don't understand is this: violence is the only logical end of the road for their ideas. Free men, men of self-esteem, do not like their lives and property to be sacrificed on the altar of the collective (the State). They do not like to be stolen from. They don't like their lives to be proscribed by the state. They laugh at the foolish utterances of bureaucrats. They resist. So the only alternative is for the government to do the only thing it can do—wield force. Socialism did not fail in Soviet Russia and Nazi Germany because it was not implemented properly—it failed because it is as evil in theory as it was in practice.

FDR was no Stalin, but he was influenced by the same ideas. And even in America, he was able to implement many of them. In fact, it was the sainted Franklin Delano Roosevelt who is most responsible for America's abandonment of our 150 year history of free enterprise. It was Franklin Delano Roosevelt who cemented the ideas of Karl Mark and Joseph Stalin into the American system… therefore making it a system that is now not even remotely American.

Roosevelt's New Deal was a planned economy with an outward façade of private ownership. But ownership of private property was reduced to a mere title on a legal document. Because of the power Roosevelt was willing to yield under the guise of the economic "emergency," that he in large part created, everyone in the society was subservient to the state.

Roosevelt's major New Deal programs—the National Recovery Act (NRA) and the Agricultural Adjustment Act (AAA)—were almost replicas of the Italian fascist model. Only the Supreme Court decisions of 1935, declaring the NRA and AAA unconstitutional, saved America from a comprehensive fascist future.

For his NRA program, Roosevelt and his "brain trust" developed a "Blue Eagle" insignia, which they launched with a parade on 5th Avenue (again taking propaganda lessons from the communists). Any American citizen who did not do his patriotic duty by supporting the NRA and its Blue Eagle soon found himself on the receiving end of FDR's thugs. The Blue Eagle was a fascist-like symbol of compliance with the government's dictates. FDR said on the radio that "soldiers wear a bright badge to be sure that comrades do not fire on comrades. Those who cooperate in this program must know each other at a glance. That bright badge is the Blue Eagle." And, added Roosevelt's NRA Director Hugh Johnson, may "God have mercy on anyone who attempts to trifle with that bird."

In his book, *The Roosevelt Myth*, author John T. Flynn shows that Johnson wasn't kidding. There were police raids of factories, as workers were lined up and interrogated. Why? To make sure they weren't working overtime and weren't accepting less than the government-approved minimum! Consumers were arrested for paying less than the approved minimum prices. One unfortunate New Jersey tailor, Jack Magid, was arrested and jailed for ignoring the diktats of the Blue Eagle. His crime? He was charging 35 cents instead of 40 cents to press a pair of pants.

In time, the NRA became difficult to enforce, since black markets sprung up everywhere in every industry. FDR's crackdown intensified, with nighttime raids on factories, and bureaucrats chopping down doors with axes to make sure that no one was sewing clothes. The NRA staff ballooned from 60 employees to 6,000 at the national level.

All of it was based on the ridiculous premise that by boosting prices at the point of a gun they were somehow boosting production, when of course the exact opposite is true. Finally, the Supreme Court came to the rescue and declared the whole thing Unconstitutional.

Once they were defeated in their drive for fascist-style planning, the social engineers retreated into piecemeal planning. If you're going to cook a frog and don't want him to jump out of the pot, just turn up the temperature bit by bit so he doesn't feel it, right?

Regulatory agencies proliferated. Public-works projects were created in abundance. Fiscal and monetary policy was implemented. Economic subsidies and political privileges were provided to increasing numbers of special-interest groups.

Even worse, with his "four freedoms," Roosevelt perverted the Founding Fathers concept of rights by changing it from "I have a right to act in pursuit of my happiness as long as I don't infringe on the rights of others," into "other people must provide for my needs."

Take, for example, Roosevelt's Economic Bill of Rights. Here is a telling excerpt from his January 11, 1944 message to Congress on the State of the Union…

"The Economic Bill of Rights"

> It is our duty now to begin to lay the plans and determine the strategy for the winning of a lasting peace and the establishment of an American standard of living higher than ever before known. We cannot be content, no matter how high that general standard of living may be, if some fraction of our people—whether it be one-third or one-fifth or one-tenth—is ill-fed, ill-clothed, ill-housed, and insecure.

> This Republic had its beginning, and grew to its present strength, under the protection of certain inalienable political rights—among them the right of free speech, free press, free worship, trial by jury, freedom from unreasonable searches and seizures. They were our rights to life and liberty.
>
> As our nation has grown in size and stature, however—as our industrial economy expanded—these political rights proved inadequate to assure us equality in the pursuit of happiness.
>
> We have come to a clear realization of the fact that true individual freedom cannot exist without economic security and independence. "Necessitous men are not free men."
>
> People who are hungry and out of a job are the stuff of which dictatorships are made.
>
> In our day these economic truths have become accepted as self-evident. We have accepted, so to speak, a second Bill of Rights under which a new basis of security and prosperity can be established for all—regardless of station, race, or creed.
>
> Among these are:
>
> The right to a useful and remunerative job in the industries or shops or farms or mines of the nation;
>
> The right to earn enough to provide adequate food and clothing and recreation;
>
> The right of every farmer to raise and sell his products at a return which will give him and his family a decent living;
>
> The right of every businessman, large and small, to trade in an atmosphere of freedom from unfair competition and domination by monopolies at home or abroad;
>
> The right of every family to a decent home;
>
> The right to adequate medical care and the opportunity to achieve and enjoy good health;
>
> The right to adequate protection from the economic fears of old age, sickness, accident, and unemployment;
>
> The right to a good education.
>
> All of these rights spell security. And after this war is won we must be prepared to move forward, in the implementation of these rights, to new goals of human happiness and well-being. America's own rightful place in the world depends in large part upon how fully these and similar rights have been carried into practice for our citizens.

This is an amazing document. It is, of course, a manifesto for socialism. The rights he cites are not rights at all. They are simply assertions that some men have a claim on the property or services of other men. For every one of them all you need to ask is this: at whose expense?

Who is to be forced to provide these things? A right to a job? A right to a decent home?

But here is the killer: this is supposedly an "Economic Bill of Rights;" yet, property rights and the right of free trade are man's only real economic rights and he doesn't even mention them! Of course, property rights are really political rights, not economic rights. There can be no such things as an economic bill of rights because that would entail violating the rights of others. (Again, that's the bogus "positive rights" assertion of the progressives).

Given all of the above, one can see the parallels to what is going on today. The similarities are indeed ominous. The idea that government should provide a "right" to a decent home is what led to things like the Community Reinvestment Act, which was the match that lit the sub-prime mortgage crisis and the real estate bubble that popped in 2008. President Obama is now approaching the end of his first (and let us pray "only") term of office and his administration has rivaled FDR's in their scope of turbo-statist activity.

Crack #3: The 1960's and the "Great Society"

And what began under Franklin Roosevelt in the 1930's and 1940's remained in place in the 1950's and 1960's. The "Great Society" programs initiated in the mid-1960s by LBJ extended and accelerated the creeping tyranny of state control through the introduction of property redistribution as a cornerstone of governmental policy. In the 19th century, the government could have been safely ignored by everyone in society except for criminals. Thanks to the progressives and the New Dealers, government was effectively king by the 1960's.

Unfortunately, just as much of the Depression generation bought into the New Deal, much of the "greatest" generation that fought World War II went along with the expansion of government programs that accelerated after America became prosperous in the decade following the War. The result is we will have perhaps one-and-a-half generations that will benefit from this "largesse" in their twilight years—particularly with the entitlement programs of Social Security and Medicare. But at what cost? At the cost of destroying the foundations of the country, ceding control over our own health care to the government, crushing our prosperity and leaving unimaginable debt to future generations. When all of the baby boomers have to be paid, the Ponzi scheme will collapse. Well, as long as you got yours I guess.

While the New Deal was spawned from the "crisis" of the Great Depression, the largest expansion of the welfare state came in the 1960s and 1970s. The irony is that until John F. Kennedys "New Frontier" and Lyndon Johnson's "Great Society" programs, poverty rates were dropping in the United States, especially for blacks, from more than thirty-three percent in the early 1950s to less than fifteen percent by the mid 1960s. In other words, economic expansion due to capitalism and the philanthropic sector it created was helping to eradicate poverty on its own.

However, within a few years of Johnson's welfare state programs, poverty rates stiffened and even rose slightly. At the same time, inner cities, which received large amounts of "redistribution" payments, began to be transformed from enclaves of growing prosperity to an urban reservation for the nation's "underclass."

Economist Walter Williams describes the differences from his own experience:

> During the 1940s, my family lived in North Philadelphia's Richard Allen housing project. Many families didn't lock doors until late at night, if ever. No one ever thought of installing bars on their windows. Hot, humid summer nights found many people sleeping outside on balconies or lawn chairs. Starting in the '60s and '70s, doing the same in some neighborhoods would have been tantamount to committing suicide. Keep in mind that the 1940s and '50s were a time of gross racial discrimination, high black poverty and few opportunities compared to today. The fact that black neighborhoods were far more civilized at that time should give pause to the excuses of today that blames today's pathology on poverty and discrimination.

Indeed, along with vast increases in welfare subsidies came accompanying expansions in unwed motherhood, drug use, crime, and overall moral decay.

Although it was clear from the start that the "Great Society" was a colossal failure, many groups of well-educated suburbanites called for its expansion. While their stated reasons were "compassion for the poor," it turned out that some of the greatest recipients of this new largesse were middle-class government employees.

In the mid-1970's, New York City's financial crisis was brought on because politicians and bureaucrats had managed to turn that magnificent city into one giant welfare state. Among some of the subsidies were tuition-free education from pre-school through graduate school, free hospitalization, and hundreds of other "benefits." Most of those "free lunches" were financed by overtaxed businesses. So many businesses left.

Once again, history is repeating itself as several prominent figures and businesses have announced they are leaving New York due to its onerous tax increases on businesses and wealthy individuals. Apparently, many politicians prefer the New York City of the 1970's.

As can be seen from the above examples, the New Deal and all of these welfare state expansions have been a colossal fraud from their inception. Their origins were cloaked in deceit and were always about the expansion of the state. Provision for the poor was always secondary to the real agenda of government domination by social and political elites. The main recipients have been friends of political leaders in the wealthy and middle classes. Far from protecting the most vulnerable in our society, the welfare state has made all of us even more vulnerable to the worst kinds of wealth redistribution, expropriation, social deterioration, and economic chaos.

As the government expands, freedom shrinks. We have now reached a point where the average salary of public sector employees is higher than the average salary of those in the private sector. In other words, the non-productive sector is sucking the life blood out of the productive sector. Not only do those working in the private sector pay the salaries of public employees and the vast army of bureaucrats in Washington, they also have to pay for lavish pensions and retirement benefits that are often paid out for decades after retirement—all paid for by taxpayers of course.

Pension and benefit costs are another reason why State governments are also going broke. In addition to our Federal government, major states like California, New York, Illinois, Ohio and New Jersey are on the verge of bankruptcy. Large cities like Los Angeles, Chicago, New York, Washington, D.C., Newark, and Detroit are facing bankruptcy as well. Why? One of the primary reasons is because the public sector pays people while they are working… and then keeps paying them for decades for not working.

And today, we have taken it one step further with Welfare expanding to huge Wall Street Firms and corporations such as General Motors. Taxpayers are now subsidizing huge industries, including businesses that have not earned a profit in a decade and likely never will. In other words, using GM as an example, your money is being stolen and given to auto workers simply so they can have a job—a job of zero productive value. The auto industry in Detroit was destroyed for a variety of reasons, not the least of which is the fact that for every current worker they have 10 non-workers receiving pension benefits.

How did that happen? Through government-enforced collective bargaining, Detroit's auto makers "agreed" to let auto workers retire with full pension and benefits after 30 years on the job, regardless of their age. In practice, that meant a worker could start at age 18, retire at 48, and spend another 30 years (or more) collecting a pension and free health care. So now, since taxpayers are the ones subsidizing both current and past workers of GM, it is you that are paying for all of this. I hope you got a thank you.

When you look at this slide into socialism over a long period of time, the changes have been incremental and often subtle. But that's how totalitarian governments work. They start out with promises of "freedom from need" and "security" and "equality of outcome." They redefine "private" and make it "public." They intervene in the economy and rig the game. They use the poor as human shields in order to advance their liberty-crushing agenda. While politicians pay lip service to the poor, what they are really doing is relentlessly consolidating their own power.

And the Founding Fathers weep at the sight of it all. They gave us a moral compass, the torch of liberty, and the roadmap to freedom and prosperity. Duped by politicians, we sold them out for the silly utopian ideas of a few old, miserable Germans and the alleged "security" that comes with the promise of thirty pieces of someone else's silver.

Intended or Unintended Consequences?

All government programs that are not for the purpose of protecting men from force and fraud are unconstitutional and a violation of individual rights. For those of us that love Liberty, the discussion is over right there. Liberty comes first always as a matter of moral principle.

But sadly, that's not even the worst of it, because these government intrusions in the private sector always achieve the opposite of what is intended. There are laws of economic cause and effect and every government intervention in the free market has unintended consequences that are detrimental in the long run. None of the Left's socialist programs work, and they always make the problem they were seeking to improve worse, not better.

However, today, given the crystal clear experiments with socialism in the 20th century, we really have to ask whether these consequences are unintended at all? How could our current administration, full of such "smart" people, not understand what socialism leads to? The grim reality we all have to face is this: they DO understand what it leads to. That's why they want it. They want people dependent on government. They want control over the private sector. They want unlimited power so they can "fundamentally transform" the United States of America from a land of liberty into a euro-style socialist state run by a bureaucratic elite.

Sure, the government will "take care" of you. In return all you have to do is give them your freedom and liberty. This is the Faustian bargain the past two generations of Americans have made.

As a very astute Frenchman predicted long ago, while explaining his fears of where Democracy in America might eventually wind up…

> Above this race of men stands an immense and tutelary power, which takes upon itself alone to secure their gratifications and to watch over their fate. That power is absolute, minute, regular, provident, and mild. It would be like the authority of a parent if, like that authority, its object was to prepare men for manhood; but it seeks, on the contrary, to keep them in perpetual childhood: it is well content that the people should rejoice, provided they think of nothing but rejoicing. For their happiness such a government willingly labors, but it chooses to be the sole agent and the only arbiter of that happiness; it provides for their security, foresees and supplies their necessities, facilitates their pleasures, manages their principal concerns, directs their industry, regulates the descent of property, and subdivides their inheritances: what remains, but to spare them all the care of thinking and all the trouble of living?
>
> Thus it every day renders the exercise of the free agency of man less useful and less frequent; it circumscribes the will within a narrower range and gradually robs a man of all the uses of himself. The principle of equality has prepared men for these things; it has predisposed men to endure them and often to look on them as benefits.
>
> After having thus successively taken each member of the community in its powerful grasp and fashioned him at will, the supreme power then extends its arm over the whole community. It covers the surface of society with a network of small complicated rules, minute and uniform, through which the most original minds and the most energetic characters cannot penetrate, to rise above the crowd. The will of man is not shattered, but softened, bent, and guided; men are seldom forced by it to act, but they are constantly restrained from acting. Such a power does not destroy, but it prevents existence; it does not tyrannize, but it compresses, enervates, extinguishes, and stupefies a people, till each nation is reduced to nothing better than a flock of timid and industrious animals, of which the government is the shepherd.
>
> *— Alexis De Tocqueville, Democracy in America*

Tocqueville uncannily predicted the mechanics of the modern welfare state or “stealth socialism.” But what about the American people themselves? Are we really ready to be treated like children and turned into sheep?

You would think that even with a rudimentary understanding of socialism and the graphic history of its results in the past century through both World Wars and the Cold War, plus the current collapse of the post-war European welfare states, people would have enough evidence to reject it out of hand.

Yet they don’t. In fact, today we are seeing an unprecedented call for big government by a vast segment of the population, along the lines of the New Deal and the Great Society. Marx’s ghost still haunts us, clanking his chains, and leaving a trail of misery and tyranny behind him. Or as Ayn Rand once said, “socialism may be dead, but its corpse is sure rotting up the place.”

How can that possibly be? How can we be following this path here in the land of the free?

To uncover the answer to that we still have to dig a little deeper….

CHAPTER 8

WHY LIBERTY REQUIRES REASON

Religion can never reform mankind because religion is slavery.

— Robert Green Ingersoll

It is not just the ghost of Karl Marx that is haunting America. There is yet another ghost that haunts us… an even bigger ghost… I guess we could say, the ultimate ghost. That ghost is…

GOD.

By some unaccountable infatuation, religious faith has been and is considered to be of immense importance by many modern Americans. The idea of living and dying without the aid of superstitious belief horrifies some. All religions are based on the idea that God will eternally reward the true believer, and eternally damn anyone who doubts—so most people are "god fearing" believers.

However, to a growing number of Americans, religion is nothing more than primitive superstition, combined with a transparent attempt by some men to control others by wielding eternal carrots and sticks and making claims to "divine knowledge."

Throughout the ages, religion has had one mortal enemy: REASON.

Nothing was considered so pleasing to god as a man who totally denied the authority of his own mind. The priests of all of the various sects love those who check their brains at the door before they enter the Church.

Having grown up in a religious family, I understand why people are drawn to religion. For starters, people need moral guidance—people want to be good. Life is full of choices and humans need a way to navigate through life making wise choices, and distinguishing right from wrong.

Another reason is for comfort. Life can be very difficult and often filled with struggle, hardships and tragedy. Religion provides comfort by convincing people that, even when bad things happen, everything is "god's will," and there is some higher purpose that we humans simply can't understand. That is comforting to some people. Comfort and fellowship is also provided through a sense of community in belonging to your church. And yes, there is some great and uplifting music to be found in many Churches.

A final reason is that many people find the idea of death simply unbearable. Religion promises immortality and a future life of ease, comfort, and bliss (if you accept and abide by the teachings that is; otherwise there is a different kind of afterlife in store for you).

The need for moral guidance, a desire to strive for the highest and best, the need for community and fellowship and the desire for comfort and immortality are all very powerful human needs and desires. Those who scoff at religion would do well to consider them in understanding why religion still remains such a powerful force in the world— despite the fact that no religion has ever produced one shred of evidence in support of its beliefs.

Having granted the above, let me next ask this: have those of you who are religious ever taken the time to really investigate the claims of your religion and think things through?

Have you ever had a look under the hood?

Is comfort more important to you than truth?

Does morality really consist in obeying the alleged dictates of ghosts as conveyed by men?

Could infants really be stained with "sin" just by virtue of having been born?

Would a just god really condemn anyone to eternal torment in hell?

If an omnipotent and omniscient god is to receive credit for the good things that happen, why doesn't he likewise get the blame when bad things happen?

Further, would it matter to you if your beliefs were undermining the foundations of your country and jeopardizing your children's future?

Would it matter to you if you discovered that your deepest beliefs were shared by your avowed political enemies?

Like socialism, religious belief is incompatible with Liberty and therefore incompatible with the American Ideal.

But unlike the men of faith, I don't expect anyone to believe that just because I've asserted it; so please allow me to make my case…

Faith vs. Reason

Contrary to what most conservatives say, America was not founded on Christian values (i.e., faith, self-sacrifice, turn-the-other-cheek pacifism, superstition, happiness in "another world"), it was founded on Enlightenment values (reason, individualism, science, the pursuit of happiness in this world).

Most fundamentally, it was founded on the rock of Reason, not the quicksand of Faith.

Whether someone believes in god or not is really just a question at the tip of an iceberg. Below the surface, there are more fundamental things to consider. For example, does the religious believer have reasons for their belief? What are they? What is the evidence?

But even deeper, what is the nature of evidence in general?

When we talk about concepts like faith and reason, we are talking about the field of philosophy called epistemology. Epistemology seeks to answer the question: "how do we know what we know?" Does man acquire knowledge by a process of reason—or by sudden revelation from a supernatural power?

Since confusion is the enemy of purposeful thought, it's important that we define our terms.

Reason is the faculty that acquires knowledge based on cognition and the evidence of the senses; as opposed to feelings or "divinely inspired" ideas. Reason demands facts and evidence and uses a process of logic.

Faith is a word that can have many meanings in common usage, depending on the context. When people use the word faith, they most commonly mean a conviction or a belief that is supported by experience or evidence. You might say, "I have faith in my husband to do the right thing." Why? Because you know him and he has always done the right thing in the past. Or you may have "faith" in a doctor who's performing surgery on you. Why? Because you checked out her record and she's performed the same operation dozens of times with positive results. Using the word faith in that way is not what is meant by faith for purposes of philosophy or religion.

When speaking about religious faith, we are talking about believing something without reason or evidence, or even despite evidence to the contrary.

Religionists know that they have no more knowledge of god, or what happens after we die, than does a chimpanzee, so they say that in order to believe their fantastic claims you need to have "faith." In other words, they want you to stop thinking and simply take their word for it.

The Christian Father Tertullian goes even further, stating that Christians should believe certain claims *because* they fly in the face of reason:

> And the Son of God died; it is by all means to be believed, because it is absurd. And He was buried and rose again; the fact is certain because it is impossible.

The trouble with that Father, as Voltaire pointed out, is that "if we believe in absurdities we shall commit atrocities."

Now, once you have "faith," and you believe these absurdities, what does religion teach you to do?

The religionists tell you there is a great ghost in the sky who is all-knowing, all-powerful, and all-wise. They tell you he is the creator of the universe, the ultimate source of truth and the giver of moral law. They tell you that you are nothing, God is everything, and your duty is to obey his will. They tell you that you must live to glorify him, obey his commands, believe the Bible, and accept Jesus as your lord and savior (for he sacrificed his life for you, to take away your sins and the sins of the world).

And what does god want you to do? In a word: SACRIFICE.

Religious scholars, such as the Christian Reverend John Stott explain it very plainly to us: "God's order is that we put him first, others next, self last. Sin is the reversal of that order."

Rabbi Abraham Heschel will second that, saying, "the essence and greatness of man do not lie in his ability to please his ego, to satisfy his needs, but rather in his ability to ignore his own needs; to sacrifice his own interests in the sake of the holy."

Like Christianity and Judaism, Islam is also based on sacrifice. The chief feast in the world of Islam is the Feast of Sacrifice held at Mecca during the pilgrimage and simultaneously in every Moslem community from Tangier to Timbuktu.

For these three theistic religions, this all goes back to the story of Abraham sacrificing his son on Mount Moriah in order to demonstrate his "faith" in god. And of course, that story has even older origins that stem from the blood-sacrifice of primitive people attempting to appease the "gods." This primitive and horrible idea of making sacrifices in order to show our "faith" in ghosts, phantoms, or "the holy," still haunts us in countless ways today.

Further, the Christian "men of god" will tell you that if you do not fulfill your duty to god and also accept Jesus as your personal savior, you are nothing more than kindling wood for the never-ending bonfires of hell. (In Islam, it's even more direct: submit now or die.)

I don't know about you, but to me that all sounds very similar to something we've seen here on earth many times: dictatorship through intimidation and terror.

Now, if you are an American, and thus committed to life, liberty and the pursuit of happiness here on earth, the assertions of the religionists might disturb you a bit. If you are of the curious sort, you might ask those making these claims if they have any proof or evidence to back them up. “Yes, we have a book,” they will tell you. So you read the book, and what will you find in the book?

You will find that the universe was created by god in seven days. You will learn that man was once perfect and living in a state of paradise, until Adam disobeyed God by eating fruit from the tree of knowledge. You will learn that because of that “sin,” women will bear children in pain. You will learn that the sun revolves around the earth. You will find a god that condones slavery and polygamy. You will learn that women should be serfs and slaves of their husbands. You will learn that god drowned the entire world except for eight people, killing good and innocent alike, and turned the whole world into a sea of corpses.

You will learn that after the flood he selected a band of wandering nomads called the Jews as his “chosen ones.” Although he apparently created other people too, he didn’t pay much attention to them. He was a tribal god who protected the few and despised everyone else. You will find the story of Abraham and Isaac, a father who murdered his own son to show his “love of god.” You will learn how god killed cattle with hailstones because of the sins of the Pharaoh. You will learn how he changed sticks into serpents and water into blood.

You will learn of a god who killed the firstborn of the Egyptians—the babies of poor and innocent mothers—because of the wickedness of the king. You will soon learn that the common theme is the blessedness of human sacrifice for no apparent reason other than the “glory” of god. In the 22nd chapter of Exodus, you will see god make this command: "Thou shalt not delay to offer the first of thy ripe fruits and of thy liquors: the firstborn of thy sons thou shalt give unto me."

In the book of Joshua you will read all about wars, murders and massacres. More of the same in the book of Judges, including another story involving fratricide, when Jeptha murders his daughter to please God.

The horror goes on and on. You should read it some time. If you do, you will discover three important facts: (1) The God of the Old Testament is an ignorant, malicious and vicious god; (2) It is a book of horrors written by savages; (3) Almost every fact in this “inspired” book is wrong.

As bad as the *Old Testament* is, there is another book that exceeds it in horrors: and that's the *New Testament.*

Although the four Gospels of Matthew, Mark, Luke and John are supposedly about "the one" who brought "tidings of joy," it's even worse than the Old Testament. Why do I say that? At least when old Jehovah had you dead he let you be. Jesus however, is not satisfied with that. If you cross Jesus, you will suffer eternal and never-ending pain. It's the New Testament that introduces the concept of hell and the doctrine of eternal damnation.

Think about how twisted a mind would have to be to create such a doctrine as hell with its eternal torment. Such a doctrine is even more perverse than the doctrine of Original Sin, which is perverse enough.

I won't belabor the point about the religionists' "inspired" books. Volumes and volumes have been written showing their errors and horrors. One of the best refutations of the Bible remains Thomas Paine's, *The Age Of Reason*, which every American should read. I'd also recommend Ingersoll's *Some Mistakes of Moses*.

As the saying goes, there are two kinds of people: those who believe the Bible and those who have read it.

How parents continue to subject their children to this irrationality and evil in the 21st century is beyond comprehension. How can a mother hold her newborn infant in her arms… and feel her heart filled with an emotion that words cannot express… and at the same time believe those who tell her that her innocent child is born in "sin?" How can a father look at his baby daughter with tenderness and joy, or at his son with wonder and pride, and believe this unholy lie?

Worse still, how can these same parents turn that innocent child's mind over to those who will brainwash their children by teaching them the same evil doctrine and filling their beautiful minds with superstition, lies, fear of hell and damnation, and claims of "miracles?" How can they place them in religious classes week after week where they are taught that virtue means having "faith" and believing inane nonsense without evidence… while at the same time telling him that the worst thing he can be is a "doubting Thomas," who dares to use his own mind and actually question the dogma being forced down his throat? Most children crack under this relentless brainwashing until eventually the switch is flipped and they become un-moored from reason and reality when it comes to matters of "faith." After all, they think, who are they to go against their elders, as well as 2000 years of history and all of the pomp and circumstance of the Church.

Is that not the intellectual equivalent of child abuse?

It is not just the bodies of children that have been transgressed by priests and clerics—for over two millennia now they have been doing the same thing to their minds. Who is to blame? Is it not their parents who, under peer and familial pressure, keep sending their children back to the irrational cults of Christianity, Judaism, Islam, and all the other factories of mysticism?

Why do they continue to do this? It is not because they are so convinced that theirs is the one true religion. Let's face it, if the average American Christian were born in Saudi Arabia instead of the U.S., he would be praying five times a day toward Mecca, saying, "there is no god but Allah and Mohammed is his prophet."

No, it is not because they have done an exhaustive study of all the world's religions and are convinced of the "truth" of their religion: it is because they follow blindly and engage in monumental evasions of reality and gross hypocrisy. If they do think critically and question the dogma, they don't have the courage to go against their families and society and say the religious Emperor has no clothes. At bottom, they do not have the courage to preserve the veracity of their own minds and follow the dictates of their own reason. The brainwashing at an early age does a thorough job to most, so they stay in the cult and rationalize it all away. And so the cycle goes on and on, generation after generation.

I say it's high time we stop beating our children with the bones of our ignorant and misguided ancestors. We can do better than to cling to these primitive books and their savage creeds, can't we?

In point of fact, by employing Reason, we are doing better and mankind is slowly but steadily moving toward the light and becoming less superstitious with each passing century. We are writing what the great Ingersoll called, the real Bible…

> For thousands of years men have been writing the real Bible, and it is being written from day to day, and it will never be finished while man has life. All the facts that we know, all the truly recorded events, all the discoveries and inventions, all the wonderful machines whose wheels and levers seem to think, all the poems, crystals from the brain, flowers from the heart, all the songs of love and joy, of smiles and tears, the great dramas of Imagination's world, the wondrous paintings, miracles of form and color, of light and shade, the marvelous marbles that seem to live and breathe, the secrets told by rock and star, by dust and flower, by rain and snow, by frost and flame, by winding stream and desert sand, by mountain range and billowed sea.
>
> All the wisdom that lengthens and ennobles life, all that avoids or cures disease, or

conquers pain—all just and perfect laws and rules that guide and shape our lives, all thoughts that feed the flames of love, the music that transfigures, enraptures and enthralls the victories of heart and brain, the miracles that hands have wrought, the deft and cunning hands of those who worked for wife and child, the histories of noble deeds, of brave and useful men, of faithful loving wives, of quenchless mother-love, of conflicts for the right, of sufferings for the truth, of all the best that all the men and women of the world have said, and thought and done through all the years.

These treasures of the heart and brain—these are the Sacred Scriptures of the human race.

— Robert G. Ingersoll

If we are going to worship, let's worship the true and the good. Let's worship things that are REAL.

Some, most notably Thomas Aquinas, have attempted to reconcile reason and faith, but all such attempts have failed, because they are logically impossible—and everyone who has had any experience with religion knows it deep down. You can't put out the sun and then honestly believe that it's still shining.

Enter The Age Of Reason

"One hundred years ago, our fathers retired the gods from politics." So said Colonel Robert G. Ingersoll on July 4, 1876 in Peoria, Illinois, during his Centennial oration. Ingersoll was referring to the drafting of the Declaration of Independence one hundred years prior.

Calling the United States Constitution "the grandest, the bravest, and the profoundest political document that was ever signed by the representative of a people," and "the embodiment of physical and moral courage and of political wisdom," he went on to eloquently pay tribute to the first document in the history of man that sought to uphold the rights of the individual and strictly limit the functions of government.

In that speech he also said, "With one blow, with one stroke of the pen, they struck down all the cruel, heartless barriers to aristocracy, that priest-craft, that king-craft had raised between man and man." Ingersoll, once arguably the most famous American of his day (and virtually unknown today) would roll over in his grave if he knew the extent to which the Declaration of Independence and the Constitution have been undermined today. And of course, the Founding Fathers that he spoke of so reverently would be rolling with him.

Ingersoll, like our Founding Fathers, knew that men could not be truly free if they believed in the supernatural and felt they were under an obligation to worship and obey a dictator in the sky.

At the time of Ingersoll's speech in 1876, religion was on the decline in America and probably at its lowest point. The Enlightenment influence had been consistently growing through the 18th and early 19th centuries. It's no coincidence that America's greatest period of invention, creation and technological advances began during that period. Americans of that time believed in the "liberty of hand and brain" as Ingersoll put it.

The eighteenth century was called the Age of Reason because it was the apex of the Enlightenment. It was the end result of more than four hundred years of efforts to secularize the western mind and liberate it from its medieval shackles.

After centuries of groping in darkness… of believing in ghosts, goblins, phantoms and gods… of cringing and crawling before priests and kings… by the 18th century, men were taking for granted that the universe was intelligible through reason and science. It was the age of Newton's influence in Science, and Locke in Philosophy.

The supernatural had lost. Those who pushed angels and devils, heavens and hells, and told the people to tremble in fear and "believe" without question had lost. Ignorance and superstition had lost. The idea of sacrificing this world for an alleged "higher" world had lost.

Despite the best efforts of religionists to chain the mind and the body through intimidation and torture, the mind was winning. Everywhere there was invention, exploration and discovery. The old beliefs began to be looked upon as savage and absurd. People were becoming tired of barbarian bibles and primitive creeds.

A respect for Reason animated Western Culture. The people were determined to sweep aside the errors of the past and begin anew. Men understood that if they applied intelligence and reason to the problems of living, nature could be mastered and shaped in ways that served human needs. Thought became a beacon of hope rather than a source of sin.

The result was the overwhelming self-confidence of the period. Men were animated with the notion that there were no limits to the achievements and advances that could be gained through science and pursuing knowledge. The primordial concepts of original sin and man's innate depravity were rejected. They were replaced by a view of man as potentially perfectible through education and knowledge.

In a letter of advice to his nephew, Peter Carr, who was entering college

> Fix reason firmly in her seat and call to her tribunal every fact, every opinion. Question with boldness even the existence of a God; because, if there be one, he must more approve of the homage of reason, than that of blindfolded fear.

Could we improve upon this advice for our own children? I don't see how. Reason—your reason—should guide your judgment. But you must make sure that you gather all facts and opinions from both sides of any question before making your judgment.

Seconding Jefferson a century later, Robert Ingersoll put it this way, "It has always seemed absurd to suppose that a god would choose for his companions, during all eternity, the dear souls whose highest and only ambition is to obey."

And that gets to the heart of the matter when considering how religious belief relates to politics.

Religionists make assertions, claims—and then demands—saying that it is "god almighty" who demands whatever they are pronouncing. The trouble is, since nobody has seen this god, the demands they make and pronounce from on high look suspiciously like the demands of men—men who are not-so-almighty, but who do have some very earthly agendas.

As a matter of fact, this almighty "god" they speak of looks suspiciously like the creation of men himself, does he not?

Elihu Palmer, an American author of the pre-revolutionary period who founded a newspaper called "The Temple of Reason," wrote, "It has hitherto been deemed a crime to think. But at last men have escaped from the long and doleful night of Christian rule, with its frenzy, its religious fanaticism, and its mad enthusiasm. At last men have grasped the unlimited power of human reason. Reason, which every kind of supernatural theology abhors. Reason, which is the glory of our nature."

It was in this atmosphere—an atmosphere that viewed man as a rational, self-sufficient, potentially noble being—that the United States of America was conceived.

"We have it in our power to begin the world over again," wrote Thomas Paine. The Founders were very much aware of what they were doing. They knew that they had a unique historical opportunity to found a country on the right principles—Enlightenment principles—based in reason and liberty.

"Let us learn from the errors of other nations, and lay hold of the present opportunity to begin government at the right end," said Paine in Common Sense. Jefferson said, "the first was a government of kings, the second of priest-craft, and the third of Reason."

After the Revolution, Thomas Paine published his devastating critique of the Bible and organized religion, *The Age of Reason*, declaring, "I do not believe in the creed professed by the Jewish Church, by the Roman Church, by the Greek Church, by the Turkish Church, by the Protestant Church, nor by any church that I know of. My own mind is my own church." And he added, "All national institutions of churches, whether Jewish, Christian, or Turkish, appear to me none other than human inventions, set up to terrify and enslave mankind, and monopolize power and profit."

Nobody did more to spur the Revolution than Tom Paine, from his *Common Sense* in 1775 to *The American Crisis*, written alongside Washington during the darkest days of the war. But despite their enormous debt to him, the religious "conservatives" of the day turned their back on Tom Paine after he came out with *The Age Of Reason*. It remains one of our greatest injustices that he died in ignominy and not as a national hero.

Colonel Ethan Allen, Revolutionary hero of the battle of Fort Ticonderoga, titled his book on religion, *Reason Is The Only Oracle Of Man*. In the preface to his book he wrote, "I am no Christian, except infant baptism make me one." He added, "prayer is no part of rational religion, nor did reason ever dictate it."

What is so important about this emphasis on reason? Simply this: holding reason as an absolute necessarily means a rejection of faith (and therefore a rejection of religion). It's important to understand that, although many Founders considered themselves Christians, the founding of The United States of America was politically secular in nature.

Most of the Founders did not reject the idea of the supernatural completely. Some were Christians and others were Deists, who believed there was an impersonal creator who "got things going" in the same way a watchmaker builds a watch and then lets it run. We also need to keep in mind that, during their time, blasphemy was still considered a crime punishable by death in many of the colonies. Publicly, they were not free to speak their true thoughts and often paid lip service to God in political speeches, while saying otherwise in their private correspondence.

Others such as Paine, Jefferson, Franklin, and Ethan Allen were atheists in the strict sense of the term (a-theism, simply means lacking in theistic belief). Most of them clearly rejected theism—the idea that there is an omnipotent and omniscient god that controls the world and the actions of men on a personal level.

Jefferson was so offended by the absurd miracles and supernatural claims in the Bible, he stripped out all of what he considered Jesus' best teachings and created his own mini Bible, free of any supernatural references.

We can debate about how "Christian" many of the founders were, but the key point is this: Jefferson, along with many of the other most influential Founders, did not believe the Bible was true or "inspired."

Furthermore, when the Founders wrote the Constitution, they specified that "no religious test shall ever be required as a qualification to any office or public trust under the United States." (Article 6, section 3).

This provision was radical in its day. It gave equal citizenship to believers and non-believers alike. They wanted to ensure that no single religion could make the claim of being the official "state religion," as existed in England.

In fact, nowhere in the Constitution does it mention religion, except in exclusionary terms. The words "Jesus Christ, Christianity, Bible, and God" are never mentioned in the United States Constitution—not once.

If the Founders believed man's rights came from god, why did they leave him out of our Constitution entirely?

Where Rights Actually Come From

Despite the fact that the Bible is demonstrably not "inspired," and there is no evidence for the existence of any supernatural being, conservatives and other religionists make the claim that man's rights come from "god." They ignore the fact that god is not mentioned in the Constitution, but point to the Declaration, which says, "men are endowed by their creator" with certain inalienable rights.

Notice however, that in the Declaration they did not use the term God or mention Jesus Christ. They used the impersonal term of "creator," which can be taken to be a supernatural being or it could be taken to mean Nature.

In fact, the Enlightenment concept was based on "natural rights" theory, meaning that rights are the product of nature. But what exactly does that mean? Does it mean that the wind whispers in a man's ear "you have a right to life and liberty..."

No, they were not talking about nature in that sense. They were not talking about the metaphysical world or external nature. They were talking about man's internal nature, i.e., man's identity. What type of being is man?

If we return to John Quincy Adams' quote from Chapter One, we can see this view expressed clearly:

> There were spirits capable of tracing civil government to its foundation in the moral and physical nature of man; but conquest and servitude were so mingled up in every part of the social existence of the nation, that these had become vitally necessary to them. [Italics mine.]

The foundation for political rights is to be found in the moral and physical nature of man.

And what is man's nature? What distinguishes man from animals, rocks, and trees?

Is it not our ability to REASON? Man is the rational animal. He does not act on instinct—he survives and flourishes by thinking.

And part of the evolution of that thinking was man's development of the concept of rights. In other words, rights are a human concept. They are moral principles that define how humans should behave in a society. It logically follows then, that in order to have rights, you must be able to understand the concept so you can respect the rights of others. You must have a conceptual faculty. Which is why humans have rights and animals, rocks, and trees do not.

One of the best definitions of rights is provided by Ayn Rand:

> Rights are a moral concept—the concept that provides a logical transition from the principles guiding an individual's actions to the principles guiding his relationship with others—the concept that preserves and protects individual morality in a social context—the link between the moral code of a man and the legal code of a society, between ethics and politics. Individual rights are the means of subordinating society to moral law.

In all of the books of the Bible, there is no talk of man's inalienable rights. The one positive idea found in the New Testament was Jesus' insistence that each person's individual soul has value. That was good. But he ruined it in the next breath by claiming that very same soul was born depraved and would wind up in eternal torment unless they saw himself, the magnificent Jesus Christ, as "the way, the truth and the light." Talk about an ego.

Throughout the Bible, there is no talk of Liberty, there is no talk of the proper principles of a free society. There is nothing even remotely as clear or well-reasoned as the Lockean concept of the individual's right to life, liberty, and property. Yet, religionists still claim that the Bible is the source of moral law and rights come from "god."

Here is the problem with that: what if someone's god tells him something different from what your "good" god tells you? What if one's god tells him to do things that are immoral by rational standards? What if the god of a "man of faith" tells him that women should wear veils at all times or else be stoned to death? What if his god tells him that homosexuals should be put to death? What if one's god tells him he will gain paradise by flying planes into buildings and killing infidels?

How do you Christians combat that? After all, radical Islamists are men of "faith" too and therefore their appeals to faith are just as valid as yours, are they not? How can you prove otherwise?

The truth is, you combat it by simply dismissing their god and their beliefs as irrational. And if you can understand the reason why you dismiss the injunctions of the Muslim god, then you can certainly understand why rational men dismiss the injunctions of your Christian god. The source of both beliefs—FAITH—is one and the same.

It is true that the Christian world was influenced by the Renaissance and Enlightenment and went through a period of reformation that the Muslim world has not. However, that's not an argument for faith and religion—it's an argument for reason and secularism.

No, rights are not the product of faith. Rights are the product of reason and the facts of reality. They come from "the moral and physical nature of man." Ghosts had nothing whatsoever to do with it.

As a matter of fact, it could be argued that rights were conceived of in order to protect the individual from the men of faith—specifically the Christian faith, which was dominant in the West. Prior to the Enlightenment, it was the Christian nations that were the most warlike. Like Islam today, the early Christians believed they had the exact truth from god, so they had no respect for the rights of non-Christians and committed barbarity after barbarity, atrocity after atrocity. "Believing himself to be the slave of God, he imitates the master, and of all tyrants, the worst is a slave in power."

Neither Christianity nor Islam need to be "reformed"—it would be better if they were just repudiated and abandoned.

CHAPTER 9
AMERICA'S ACHILLES HEEL

When plunder becomes a way of life for a group of men together in a society, they create for themselves in the course of time, a legal system that authorizes it and a moral code that glorifies it. — Frédéric Bastiat

In modern times, there are two primary forces that have been opposing the Founders' ideas of reason and liberty… the best known symbols of these ideas are Jesus Christ and Karl Marx as we've been discussing.

If you've ever wondered how people from both the right and the left could vote for politicians that are clearly statist, even after our experiences with socialism-communism-fascism in the 20th century, here's the reason why: contrary to popular belief, religion and socialism, and thus Jesus and Karl, are essentially two sides of the same coin.

What is that coin? That coin is the morality of Altruism. Altruism is the "moral code" that glorifies plunder as a way of life. How? By justifying it through appeals to self-sacrifice and duty. Altruism is the Achilles heel of America.

To truly understand why this country got so far off course, we have to look at and question the prevailing morality of altruism (i.e., sacrifice yourself for the good of others) that is sold by both Christianity and Socialism. When Mr. Obama says, "we are our brother's keepers," that is a Christian maxim. Christianity teaches that it is moral to sacrifice for others and immoral to think about yourself and act in your own self-interest.

Well, that Christian teaching is exactly consistent with the Communist saying "from each according to his ability, to each according to his need." The sad fact of the matter is that socialism is simply a secularized version of Christianity.

In Communism, the god of the sky is replaced by the god of the state and the same ethics remains. An ethics that says self-sacrifice is the moral ideal. It says suffering is the moral ideal. It says you should sacrifice here on earth if you want to be rewarded after you die. The ultimate expression of this was Jesus' suffering and death on the cross for the transgressions of others (for the "sins of mankind.") In the atheistic Communist version, the concept of heaven is replaced by the earthly "utopia" that will soon come about if we would only collectively sacrifice for others and be subservient to the wise, all-powerful state.

Consider the following quotes…

> Sell all that you have and distribute to the poor, and you will have a treasure in heaven; and come, follow Me.
>
> —Luke, 18:18
>
> All that believed were together, and had all things in common; And sold their possessions and goods, and parted them to all men, as every man had need.
>
> —Acts 2:44-45
>
> Neither was there any among them that lacked: for as many as were possessors of lands or houses sold them, and brought the prices of the things that were sold, and laid them down at the apostles' feet: and distribution was made unto every man according as he had need.
>
> — Acts 4:34-35
>
> Let no man seek his own! But evert man another's wealth.
>
> — I Corinthians, 10. 24.
>
> You shall lend not only to the well-to-do, who can also lend to you at some time, but also to him from whom there is no prospect of this, to the poor. – Luke
>
> From each according to his ability, to each according to his needs.
>
> – Karl Marx

Then there is the New Testament story of poor Ananias and Sapphira, who sold a piece of property but only gave the community a portion of the proceeds, keeping some of it for themselves. When Peter confronts them about their "selfishness," they both fall down and die. In other words, they were struck dead by God. Killing bourgeoisie land owners who fail to give all of their money to the community? That's not merely communism, that's Stalinism.

Communism and Animosity Toward The Rich Of The Early Christians

The social organization of the early Christians—as presented in the New Testament—was one of "communism." It was not Communism in the modern sense, but small "c" communism, or consumption communism. Jesus regarded himself as the prophet of the coming Kingdom of God, which according to ancient prophecy would bring an end to all earthly suffering and therefore economic cares. (Many of his followers view Obama in similar fashion).

Jesus' followers had "no need for the morrow." They were getting ready to eat and drink at the Lord's table. All they had to do was wait and prepare for the big day, in the same way that more recent cults waited around for the "mother ship." It's important to understand this, because it explains why Jesus offered few guidelines for living here on earth. There are no political or economic aspects to his teachings. Why would there be? Christ and his disciples lived in daily expectation of salvation. This is why in the Sermon on the Mount he tells them not to worry about food, drink, or clothing; he exhorts them not to sow or reap, not to labor or spin. They are getting ready to join the great Welfare State in the sky.

While they were waiting, they decide to divvy up all the goods – "unto each, according as anyone had need." Sound familiar? This is a primitive form of communism, it's not socialism because there is no thought given to the problems of production. They weren't worried about production at all because they thought they were going to be "saved" at any moment.

This way of life is of course, unsustainable, and the primitive Christians ran into a problem when the mother ship never arrived. Eventually, the idea of imminent salvation morphed into the concept of the Last Judgment. Realizing they were going to be around for a while, the early Christian congregations gradually began to adapt themselves to the prevailing social order of the Roman Empire in order to survive. Their members realized they would actually need to work and produce after all if they wanted to eat.

By understanding the above, we can see why there really were no social teachings in primitive Christianity, during the time of the historical Jesus. The leader and his followers were waiting to be beamed up at any moment. In other words, they were quite insane. Although it's an error to say that Jesus taught socialism as administered by the state, there are other aspects to his teaching that grease the skids for statism and encourage nihilism. As Ludwig von Mises explains in his book, *Socialism:*

> The expectation of God's own reorganization when the time came and the exclusive transfer of all action and thought to the future Kingdom of God, without offering anything to replace it, made Jesus' teachings utterly negative. He rejects everything that exists without offering anything to replace it. He arrives at dissolving all existing social ties. The disciple shall not merely be indifferent to supporting himself, shall not merely refrain from work and dispossess himself of all goods, but he shall hate "father, mother, and wife, and children, and brethren, and sisters, yea, and his own life.

Jesus exhibits a disdain for this world and of mankind. He wants to destroy social ties and even exhorts his followers to "hate" their loved ones and even their own lives. Because of his belief in the superiority of the coming Kingdom of God, he attacks everything that exists, including the love of family and the institution of private property.

Mises continues, "everything may be destroyed because God in his omnipotence will rebuild the future order. No need to scrutinize whether anything can be carried over from the old to the new order, because the new order will arise without human aid. It demands therefore from its adherents no system of ethics, no particular conduct in any positive direction. Faith and faith alone, hope, expectation – that is all he needs."

Faith and hope. Sounds like our new socialist Messiah does it not?

The parallels between primitive Christianity and modern socialism and communism are obvious. Like the early Christians, Socialists and Communists also wish to destroy everything that exists because they regard it as bad and want to "remake it" as Mr. Obama repeats often. As he said, he wants to "fundamentally transform the United States of America." Where they differ is that modern socialists seek to build the new order, their new Kingdom or vision of the anointed, here on earth.

Other aspects of Christianity consistent with socialism are its lack of support for private property and its animosity toward the rich. You can look long and hard but you will not find a single passage in the New Testament that upholds an inalienable right to private property. You can find some things, based on Jewish teaching, upholding property in the Old Testament, but that tells us nothing about the Christian view.

What you will find in the New Testament is a searing animosity toward the rich. The rich man is condemned merely because he is rich, the beggar is praised merely because he is poor. Jesus makes no effort to understand how the rich man came to be rich; it matters not to him whether it was through honest work and frugality. Nor does he inquire about how the poor man came to be poor; did he suffer hardship and tragedy, or was he a lazy drunkard? None of that matters to Jesus. According to him, in God's Kingdom the poor shall be rich, but the rich will be made to suffer.

When you consider the collectivism, the hatred of the rich, the pervasive calls for self-sacrifice, and the outright denigration of this world in the Bible (i.e., prove your love of God by murdering your son; the meek shall inherit the earth; it's easier for a camel to pass through the eye of a needle than for a rich man to enter heaven; it's better to give than to receive; god sacrificed his only son to take away the sins of the world, etc., etc., ad nauseum), the Bible can properly be viewed as a socialist manifesto.

Another example of the communism that results from Christianity is the story of the Pilgrims and the first Thanksgiving. Contrary to the distortions and make-believe our children are taught in grade school, Thanksgiving is not about Squanto teaching the helpless Pilgrims how to feed themselves. The real history of the Mayflower Pilgrims was recounted by their leader, William Bradford (1590-1657) in his book *Of Plymouth Plantation*, completed in 1647.

Yes, Bradford does recount how Squanto showed the Pilgrims how to "set" corn, which was a new crop they were unfamiliar with. In return, the Pilgrims introduced the Indians to the "hoe" which allowed them to grow more corn than they had ever seen before. But the real story is about the abject failure of the colony's first attempt at social organization, which was communism, and the success and abundance they found by shifting to the more just model of capitalism based on individualism. The celebration of Thanksgiving was not about being thankful to the Indians or to a ghost in the sky—neither of which was responsible for their survival.

What was? Here is Governor Bradford in his own words (with some updated spelling and explanatory brackets):

> It may be thought strange that these people should fall to these extremities in so short a time, being left competently provided when the ship [the Mayflower] left them, and had an addition by that moyetie [portion] of corn that was got by trade, besides much they got of the Indians where they lived, by one means and other.
>
> It must needs be their great disorder, for they spent excessively whilst they had, or could get it. And after they began to come into wants, many sold away their clothes and bed coverings; others (so base were they) became servants to the Indians, and would cut them wood and fetch them water for a cap full of corn; others fell to plain stealing, both night and day, from the Indians, of which they grievously complained. In the end, they came to that misery that some starved and died with cold and hunger...
>
> All this while no supply was heard of, neither knew they when they might expect any. So they began to think how they might raise as much corn as they could, and obtain a better crop than they had done, that they might not still thus languish in misery.
>
> At length, after much debate of things, the Governor [Bradford] (with the advise of the chiefest amongst them) gave way that they should set corn every man for his own particular [plant corn on his own private land], and in that regard trust to themselves; in all other things to go on in the general way as before.
>
> And so [there was] assigned to every family a parcel of land, according to the proportion of their number for that end, only for present use (but made no division for inheritance), and ranged all boys and youth under some family. This had very good success; for it made all hands very industrious, so as much more corn was planted then otherwise would have been by any means the Governor or any other could use, and saved him a great deal of trouble, and gave far better content.
>
> The women now went willingly into the field, and took their little-ones with them to set corn, which before they would allege weakness and inability; whom to have compelled would have been thought great tyranny and oppression.
>
> The experience that was had in this common course and condition, tried sundry years, and

> that amongst godly and sober men, may well evince the vanity of that conceit of Plato's and other ancients applauded by some of later times — that the taking away of property, and bringing in communities into a common wealth, would make them happy and flourishing, as if they were wiser than God.
>
> For this community (so far as it was) was found to breed much confusion and discontent, and retard much employment that would have been to their benefit and comfort. For the young-men that were most able and fit for labor and service did repine [complain] that they should spend their time and strength to work for other men's wives and children, without any recompense [payment].
>
> The strong, or man of parts, had no more in division [in amount] of victails [food] and clothes, than he that was weak and not able to do a quarter the other could; this was thought injustice. The aged and graver men to be ranked and equalized in labors, and victails, clothes, etc., with the meaner and younger sort, thought it some indignity and disrespect unto them.
>
> And for men's wives to be commanded to do service for other men, as dressing their meat, washing their clothes, etc., they deemed it a kind of slavery, neither could many husbands well brook it.
>
> Upon the point all being to have alike, and all to do alike, they thought themselves in the like condition, and have as good as another; and so, if it did not cut off those relations that God hath set amongst men, yet it did at least much diminish and take of the mutual respects that should be preserved amongst them.
>
> And would have been worse if they had been men of another condition. Let none object this is men's corruption, and nothing to the course itself. I answer, seeing all men have this corruption in them, God in his wisdom saw another course fitter for them...
>
> By the time harvest was come [fall 1623], instead of famine, now God gave them plenty, and the face of things was changed, to the rejoicing of the hearts of many, for which they blessed God.
>
> And the effect of their particular planting was well seen, for all had, one way and other, pretty well to bring the year about, and some of the abler sort and more industrious had to spare, and sell to others, so as any general want or famine hath not been amongst them since to this day [1647].

Despite the Governor's lip service to God (he was a Pilgrim after all), has there ever been a more effective refutation of socialism-communism and affirmation of capitalism?

The Christian ideal is one of altruistic self-sacrifice. If truly followed, all it can deliver is want just as it did in Plymouth Colony. To fully understand this and how it relates to all forms of statism, we also need to understand the roots of modern altruism.

Modern Altruism

Altruism is a philosophical term, coined by the French social theorist August Comte (1798-1857), that literally means "other-ism." Picking up where the Bible left off, Comte sought to establish a new religion of "That Great Being, Humanity," and defined altruism as living for others.

> The individual must subordinate himself to an Existence outside himself in order to find in it the source of his stability. And this condition cannot be effectually realized except under the impulse of propensities prompting him to live for others. The being, whether man or animal, who loves nothing outside himself, and really lives for himself alone, is by that very fact condemned to spend his life in a miserable alternation of ignoble torpor and uncontrolled excitement. Evidently the principal feature of Progress in living things is that the general consensus which we have seen to be the essential attribute of vitality should become more perfect. It follows that happiness and worth, as well in individuals as in societies, depend on adequate ascendancy of the sympathetic instincts. Thus the expression, Live for Others, is the simplest summary of the whole moral code of Positivism.

In Comtean terms, "living for others" does not mean being considerate to others and doing for others out of benevolence and generosity—it means *sacrificing* for others. It means holding others above yourself and doing for them until it hurts. Do not confuse altruism with compassion or sympathy.

It also does not mean taking care of your loved ones. Doing things for those we love is not a sacrifice. Since those we love are our highest values, caring about them and making them happy are entirely selfish acts. Altruism demands sacrifices for strangers—whether or not you voluntarily choose to sacrifice for them is irrelevant to the altruism peddler, as is the question of whether or not the recipient deserves your sacrifice.

As for morals, Comte declares the following:

> Over and above the several means of repressing personality, the essential condition of purification is the exertion of sympathy, which regulates individual existence by the family relations, and these again by the civic. It follows that, from every point of view, the ultimate systematisation of human life must consist above all in the development of altruism.

To Comte, personality, or the assertion of individuality, should be repressed in favor of "sympathy" for others. This of course leads to uncompromising collectivism in politics. Comte completely rejected any notion of individual rights as opposed to social duties, detested any form of free market capitalism as "modern anarchy," and envisioned a Religion of Humanity, established and enforced by the State, whose function would be to train every citizen in altruism and discourage outbreaks of "personality." It's worth noting, too, that in pressing for altruism, Comte exalted the emotions over the intellect (feelings over reason).

Notice that Comtean altruism goes far beyond the "golden rule" of loving your neighbor as yourself. As John Stuart Mill wrote of Comte's altruism:

> The golden rule of morality, in M. Comte's religion, is to live for others, "vivre pour

> autrui." To do as we would be done by, and to love our neighbour as ourself, are not sufficient for him: they partake, he thinks, of the nature of personal calculations. We should endeavour not to love ourselves at all. . . . All education and all moral discipline should have but one object, to make altruism (a word of his own coining) predominate over egoism.

The dictionary has an interesting biological definition that gets to the heart of the matter:

> Altruism: Instinctive behavior that is detrimental to the individual but favors the survival or spread of that individual's genes.

The key is this: altruism requires doing things that are detrimental to the individual.

Now, most Christians in America do NOT follow the ideal of self-abnegation or altruistic self-sacrifice. They do not take it seriously. They pursue their own happiness and try to live the American dream, not the Christian dream. But underneath there is always an unresolvable conflict and a gnawing sense of guilt.

After all, how can you enjoy your wealth when others are in need? How can you live in million dollar homes when children are starving? How can you go on vacations and trips and enjoy life when so many are suffering?

Is that really following the Christian ideal of self sacrifice? Is that really "living for others"? No, it certainly is not.

But instead of questioning the ethics of Christianity (and of altruism) and realizing that it is the primitive doctrine of self-sacrifice itself that is immoral and evil, and rejecting it, the Christian lives with that contradiction and tries to rationalize it by throwing money in collection boxes and not making so much as a peep when his money and property are looted from him by politicians.

But here is the most important point: this is why the Christian is a setup for the socialist politician. The socialist politician comes in preaching the same ethics about "helping the poor," sacrificing for the "common good," being our "brother's keeper," etc. The only difference is his call to sacrifice is in the name of "society" instead of in the name of "god," but the end result is the same.

So then, although we are already laboring half of our lives for the State, when politicians, such as our current President, says we are our brother's keepers and we can "achieve the dream" of "universal health care for all," to take but one example, if Congress expropriates trillions of dollars in taxes and enacts a hostile takeover of the health care industry, those brought up on the ethics of self-sacrifice (some influenced by Christianity, others by a very secular socialism) do not rebel as our Founding Fathers did. Instead, they say he is "inspiring," they say he is a "leader," and they roll over like sheep as the chains are placed around their necks and the manacles are forged for their own children and grandchildren.

What social system is compatible with a moral code like altruism?

> The social system based on and consonant with the altruist morality—with the code of self-sacrifice—is socialism, in all or any of its variants: fascism, Nazism, communism. All of them treat man as a sacrificial animal to be immolated for the benefit of the group, the tribe, the society, the state. Soviet Russia is the ultimate result, the final product, the full, consistent embodiment of the altruist morality in practice; it represents the only way that that morality can ever be practiced. — *Ayn Rand, Capitalism: The Unknown Ideal*

Socialist politicians know how to manipulate people by pretending that forced sacrifice for the "common good" is noble. They pull the strings of Christian self-sacrifice and Comtean altruism and both conservatives and liberals dance like puppets.

The Founders Stood For Individualism

Needless to say, this idea that it is the essence of morality to "sacrifice" yourself and your values for the sake of others is the opposite of the principle this country was founded on.

The Founders believed that the essence of morality was to declare and defend your own individual Liberty and pursue your own rational self-interest. They believed that your own individual happiness was the moral ideal.

Further, they believed that the individual had an inalienable right to pursue his or her own happiness. They believed that man was basically good and rejected the concept of original sin and the depravity of man. They believed that when men were free to pursue their own lives… their own self-interest… their own values… product achievement would be the result and the country as a whole would prosper and thrive.

That is why Jefferson penned the immortal phrase, the "pursuit of happiness" in the first place. He was talking about the right of every individual to pursue your own values, your own happiness—however you define it—so long as you respect the right of others to do the same. In other words, live and let live.

Note that in the Declaration the Founders did not say, "life, liberty, and the pursuit of the common good," or the "duty to sacrifice for society," or "life, service, and sacrifice for country."

The fact that we are all better off when we each pursue our own self-interest stems from the fact that in a free society with a division of labor you can only get what you want by providing values to others. Or, as the business and motivational speaker Zig Ziglar once put it, "you can have everything in the world you want if you just help enough other people get what they want."

Wealth is multiplied through the creation of value—you cannot multiply wealth by dividing it or redistributing it. In contrast to politicians, entrepreneurs, inventors and businessmen create wealth by adding value to the economy and improving the lives of their fellow men.

The idea that pursing self-interest was a positive thing and a requirement for human progress, was first enunciated in Adam Smith's *Wealth of Nations* in 1776. It's been borne out by the two centuries of history since. Tragically, a great many Americans don't seem to know our history, let alone understand the lessons of Liberty and the importance of defending self-interest on a moral basis. The constant "backsliding" can only be explained by the prevalence of the altruist virus in our culture.

In summary, all of the factors discussed in the last two chapters show how religion is pitted against the American Ideal in the following ways:

The irrationalism of its theology
The antipathy toward reason and the mind
Focus on a fantasy realm to the exclusion of the real world
The communistic heritage of the early Christians
The animosity toward the rich and private property
The tendency to force religious views on others
Holding altruistic self-sacrifice as a moral ideal.

All of the above oppose Liberty and play right into the hands of the Statist.

This is the reason why government has been expanding and moving constantly to the left over the past one hundred years, whether Democrats or Republicans were in power. In fact, for the past three decades, we have seen an enormous expansion of government and it has been the Republicans that have been in power. Now you understand why Republicans have been such pitiful defenders of Liberty—they don't really believe in it. They are for it and against it at the same time.

In the next chapter we'll take a closer look at the Republican record and the various flavors of conservatism in modern America.

CHAPTER 10

THE REPUBLICAN RECKONING

We might, depending on which socialists, and which neoconservatives are arguing, disagree about the details or the scope of health insurance plans; or about the level of taxation that should be imposed on corporations; or how much should go into social security... But where are the principles that separate us?"

— Irving Kristol (The "Godfather" of Neo-Conservatism)

That's exactly what I was wondering Mr. Kristol. The shared ethics between Christianity and Socialism explains why conservatives have always been wary of a social system based on self-interest (i.e., Capitalism) and have therefore been pitiful defenders of American Ideals. As we discussed in the last chapter, the shared Christian-Socialist ethic of altruism is the Achilles heel of America.

If this were not the case, then we would not be on a rocket sled to socialism right now, given the fact that Conservatives have held most of the power for the last three decades.

Consider these facts...

In 1994, the American voters elected Republican majorities in both the House and the Senate for the first time in forty years. This was said to mark the end of an era, the era of big government liberalism that had dominated American politics since FDR and the New Deal. It was the time of Newt Gingrich's "Contract With America," promising to re-limit the powers of the Federal Government and restore some of our foundational free market principles.

Up until 2008, the only Democrat to win a Presidential election in 28 years was Bill Clinton. Republicans have had control of the White House as well as Congress for most of the past three decades.

It seemed that since the election of Ronald Reagan, and the fall of the Berlin Wall, socialism had finally been discredited and we were in a new era of freedom, global capitalism and small government, with Conservative Republicans leading the way.

But things are not always what they seem.

Consider some more facts. Under George W. Bush, government spending increased faster than it did under Bill Clinton and more people worked for the federal government than at any time since the end of the cold war. During Bush's first term, total government spending skyrocketed to $2.48 trillion, an increase of 33%. That's the equivalent of $23,000 per household, the highest level since World War II. (Of course, Mr. Obama has easily outdone Mr. Bush, spending more in his first term than all Presidents from Washington through Reagan – combined.)

"Yes, but we were at war after 9-11," you say? Fair enough, let's take post 9-11 defense spending off the table completely. Domestic spending still went up 23% since Bush took office. In fact, the annualized growth rate of non-defense and non-homeland security spending more than doubled from 2.1 percent under Clinton to 4.8% under Bush.

What does increased spending mean? That's right, increased taxes. Bush did reduce some taxes in order to get the economy moving after 9-11 so you might think you paid less in taxes during the Bush years than you did under Clinton. But you would be wrong.

According to the Americans For Tax Reform, in their report titled, "The Cost of Government Day," Americans had to work 86.5 days just to pay their Federal income taxes, as compared to 78.5 days under Clinton. In other words, you were working 10.2% more for the government under Bush than Clinton. When you add state and local taxes to the mix, Americans worked for the government eight hours per day, five days a week from January 1 to July 12th each year.

But That Was Only The Beginning…

After years of compromising and "me-tooing" the Democrats on the issue of affordable home ownership and going along with liberals in supporting the quasi-government entities of Fannie Mae and Freddie Mac, the government-created housing bubble burst in the Fall of 2008.

Was the response of Bush administration to say, "look, we all screwed up." Did they explain it this way…

"This problem was created by government intervention. We politicians thought it would be a good idea for every family to own a home even if they couldn't afford standard mortgages, so we skewed the playing field by manipulating interest rates below the level of inflation… we strong-armed banks into lending to borrowers that were bad risks… we privatized profits for Fannie and Freddie but socialized their risks by putting taxpayers on the hook if they failed.

"We looked the other way and ignored the mounting debt they were piling up, even though we knew taxpayers would be holding the bag if they failed. This was all Unconstitutional and wrong and from now on we are going to stay out of manipulating the financial industry and the economy in general. We are going to get out of the social engineering game.

"There will be no bailouts of firms that gambled with other people's money and made bad decisions either. Let this be a lesson so in the future both borrowers and lenders will act more prudently. The American taxpayer will not be on the hook for your bad decisions. In America, the government does not interfere with honest business and private enterprises have to sink or swim on their own merit.

"Now, in order to get us out of this government-created pickle, here's what we're going to do: (a) cut the corporate tax rate from 35% to 10% to encourage reinvestment and job growth; (b) eliminate the capital gains tax to encourage investors, (c) initiate a flat tax rate of 15% across the board, (d) repeal Sarbanes-Oxley because it's strangling business growth; (e) eliminate the "mark to market" accounting rules; (f) drastically cut government spending at all levels; (g) begin a serious dismantling and phasing out of social security and Medicare which are not only unsustainable Ponzi schemes, they are Unconstitutional and never should have seen the light of day in America; (i) make a commitment to restoring Constitutional limitations on the federal government."

No, that was not exactly the response of the so-called "defenders" of traditional American ideals. Instead of doing anything remotely like the above, their response was to "jump the shark" and throw the country into the abyss of big government socialism, setting the precedent for our new regime.

Yes, it's true that investment banks gambled wildly and leveraged themselves to dangerous levels; however, that was not the cause of the problem. The cause was the government intervention. The banks would never have made those bets without the influence of politicians and implicit promises of "backstopping" because they were "too big to fail." For the best treatment of the issue to date, see Thomas Sowell's book, *The Housing Boom and Bust.*

Not all banks took part in the insanity. Luckily, there are still a few rational bankers remaining. One of them is John Allison, former CEO of BB&T Corp, which has been one of the few large banks capable of turning a major profit in recent years. In a 2009 interview in *National Review*, Allison said, "I think that government policy is the primary cause of the financial crisis. Government policy set up the problems we have in the real estate market, and it is the Big Kahuna in the room."

In a lecture that he presents on the subject, Allison provides a comprehensive run-down of economic-policy problems — everything from the Federal Reserve, to FDIC insurance to fair-value accounting standards to foreclosure laws and beyond. But he singles out the altruistic philosophy of government policymakers as the root cause of the financial crisis.

So, instead of owning up to the fact the government intervention caused the problem, declaring that this type of interference in free markets was a betrayal of the principles of freedom the country was founded on, and vowing to never make those mistakes again, what did Mr. Bush and the Republicans do? They panicked at the call for them to "do something," pushed through several trillion dollars in "bailouts" for Wall Street and began to nationalize private firms. This ushered in the biggest government takeover of private industry since the 1930's.

Before leaving office, Bush also paved the way for the even bigger coup that was yet to come—the multi-trillion dollar "stimulus" bill shoved down the throats of Americans at the beginning of the Obama administration. And what has been the result of that? Unemployment has gone up, our national debt has skyrocketed, the economy has not improved, and the country is littered with cheesy "Economic Recovery" road-signs. That's because government "stimulus" is not a stimulus to anything other than government.

How Could This Happen Under Conservatives?

It happened because, contrary to their claims, modern conservatives are not defenders of American Ideals. They are pretenders and charlatans. In order to understand why, let's take a brief look at a few of the flavors of modern conservatism…

There was a time when there was some linkage between the idea of American Conservatism and the ideals of the Founding Fathers. Two generations ago, Barry Goldwater wrote the following in his book, *The Conscience Of A Conservative…*

> The legitimate functions of government are actually conducive to freedom. Maintaining internal order, keeping foreign foes at bay, administering justice, removing obstacles to the free interchange of goods – the exercise of these powers makes it possible for men to follow their chosen pursuits with maximum freedom.

Now that is consistent with American Ideals. The government makes it possible "for men to follow their chosen pursuits with maximum freedom." The above is very similar to statements such as the following from Jefferson…

> A wise and frugal government, which shall restrain men from injuring one another, which shall leave them otherwise free to regulate their own pursuits of industry and improvement, and shall not take from the mouth of labor the bread it has earned. This is the sum of good government.

In a famous 1964 speech at the Republican Convention, "A Time For Choosing," Ronald Reagan said the following…

> Well I think it's time we ask ourselves if we still know the freedoms that were intended for us by the Founding Fathers. Not too long ago, two friends of mine were talking to a Cuban refugee, a businessman who had escaped from Castro, and in the midst of his story one of my friends turned to the other and said, "We don't know how lucky we are." And the Cuban stopped and said, "How lucky you are? I had someplace to escape to." And in that sentence he told us the entire story. If we lose freedom here, there's no place to escape to. This is the last stand on earth. And this idea that government is beholden to the people, that it has no other source of power except the sovereign people, is still the newest and the most unique idea in all the long history of man's relation to man. This is the issue of this election: Whether we believe in our capacity for self-government or whether we abandon the American revolution and confess that a little intellectual elite in a far-distant capitol can plan our lives for us better than we can plan them ourselves. You and I are told increasingly we have to choose between a left or right. Well I'd like to suggest there is no such thing as a left or right. There's only an up or down— up to man's age-old dream, the ultimate in individual freedom consistent with law and order, or down to the ant heap of totalitarianism. And regardless of their sincerity, their humanitarian motives, those who would trade our freedom for security have embarked on this downward course.

All of that is good. In fact, that entire speech was excellent and consistent with the basic ideas of the Founders. If only Reagan and other conservatives could have lived up to it. Conservatives have long claimed that they hold individual freedom as their ideal, but it is clearly not the ideal to which they subscribe in practice. We are indeed "losing freedom" here, and soon there will be no place to escape to—and conservatives have only themselves to blame.

The biggest trouble with the conservative betrayal of America is this: because they "appear" to be for the original American ideals in their rhetoric, when their socialist policies fail as they inevitably must, it's the American ideals of individualism and capitalism that take the blame.

The 2008 financial meltdown is a perfect case in point. It's being blamed on "deregulation" and the "laissez faire" policies of George Bush when nothing could be further from the truth. We have not had anything resembling Lasseiz Faire since before 1913—and George Bush wouldn't know Laissez Faire from Lucy Ball. Even the strong and often inspiring rhetoric of Goldwater and Reagan was always empty in the end, because religion has been the more dominant element of conservatism. For religious conservatives, their belief in their god trumps their belief in human liberty.

Intellectual Confusion Under A "Big Tent"

Unlike the modern Democrat party, which has had a consistent philosophy (Socialism), the modern Republican party is much more of a hodge-podge of competing ideologies and visions.

Modern conservatism rose in the aftermath of the New Deal and WWII as an intellectual movement that was against two primary things: communism abroad and the growing welfare state at home. The movement became a strong political coalition organized around Goldwater's campaign in 1964 and ultimately achieved success with the election of Ronald Reagan. When Reagan's policies also led to economic success for the country, it seemed that conservatives were ascendant. Indeed, the Republicans took the House and the Senate in 1994. And even though Bill Clinton was elected in 1992, he found it prudent to declare "the era of big government was over."

Not quite.

The problem stems from the fact that in order to achieve success, the conservatives built a hodge-podge coalition, not a movement driven by a unifying idea (such as a commitment to individual liberty for example). Under conservatism's "big tent," you may have a fiscal conservative whose big issues were keeping taxes low and a strong national defense, sitting next to an Evangelical Christian who has a very different agenda.

In reality, as early as 1996, the big tent was already beginning to shake. When you opened the tent, inside you would find social conservatives, fiscal conservatives, religious conservatives, compassionate conservatives, neoconservatives, paleoconservatives, libertarian-conservatives and more. Each of them driven by different ideas and pulling in different directions. Virtually none of them are truly for individualism. Of the groups, the ones that have had the most influence in recent years are the compassionate conservatives and neoconservatives.

Compassionate Conservatives

Let's start with the compassionate conservatives. What distinguishes compassionate conservatives from compassionate liberals? Not a thing – both shared the premise that we have a moral duty to love and support anyone with needs greater than our own.

The term "compassionate conservative" came to prominence during the 2000 Presidential campaign of George W. Bush. Many of the "old right" conservatives thought this was just "marketing," a way for Bush to appeal to part of the base that helped elect Bill Clinton. But no, the man actually meant it. It was and is a political philosophy.

This philosophy says that we, by way of our government, have a duty to serve those who are "in need." That's the compassionate part. It slightly differs from liberalism in that it pretends to fulfill those needs through government enforced "free market" mechanisms. That's supposedly the "conservative" part. If that sounds to you a lot like socialism (and a lot like Jesus), you are exactly right.

The ultimate goal of compassionate conservatism is to make all Americans more "compassionate" and therefore more open to socialist redistribution. This is the underlying reason for the massive growth in government spending and debt under the "compassionate conservative" George W. Bush, and the downward spiral we now find ourselves in.

In truth, neither group is truly compassionate, neither is truly charitable. Compassion and charity are virtues that depend on free will—forced charity is an oxymoron. If I see someone suffering and decide to help them of my own free will—with my own time or money—then you can say I acted charitably. However, if I see someone suffering and then I put a gun to YOUR head and force YOU to help him, neither of us is being compassionate or charitable. I am acting like a criminal and a thief and you are a victim.

Let's illustrate this with an example. Let us say that you live in Detroit and you are distraught to see how many people are living there in poverty. You believe that the most fortunate among us have a moral obligation to help those in need. So you decide to do something about it. You take a drive to Hyannisport, MA, and pay a visit to the Kennedy compound. You sneak in while nobody is there and you rob the place. You take everything you can: cash, gold, jewels, silverware, clothes, artwork. You even grab a boat for good measure. After you're done you don't feel the least bit guilty, and why should you? After all, those Kennedys have more money than god so they'll hardly miss that stuff, right?

You then go back to Detroit with all the loot, and you give all of it away! You make a big show of it, dropping cash from balcony windows... handing out gold coins to random people on the street... passing out valuable paintings to street singers begging for dollars. You even arrange to tow the yacht down Brush street and raffle it off to the person that has the least amount of money. The people LOVE you. They cannot believe what a wonderful, generous and charitable person you are. And why wouldn't they? After all, they are in desperate need, and you helped them through your heart-warming compassion and charity.

Anything wrong with this picture?

The irony here is that the above is exactly what politicians like the late Ted Kennedy spend their lives doing—they take other people's money and property through coercion and redistribute it to those they deem to be "needy." The "needy" to them are not limited to those that are truly poor either—they include banks, corporations, states, foreign countries, "green" energy companies, and a never ending stream of lobbyists and other constituencies. Pretty much anyone that will vote for them. The fact that it is done through a democratic process does not make it any less immoral than the example above. It just makes it less messy.

The Founders understood the danger of looking at government as a charity because they knew government was force. They also understood the importance of principles as well as the rapacious nature of government. A couple of memorable examples will demonstrate this…

In 1794, when Congress appropriated $15,000 for relief of French refugees who fled from insurrection in San Domingo to Baltimore and Philadelphia, an irate James Madison stood on the floor of the House to object saying…

> I cannot undertake to lay my finger on that article of the Constitution which granted a right to Congress of expending, on objects of benevolence, the money of their constituents.
>
> — James Madison, 4th Annals of Congress 179 (1794)

So what do you think? Was Mr. Madison lacking in compassion? Did he have something against French refugees? Or did he understand that charity must be left as a private matter, because he knew what would happen if government was allowed to use its power of force to redistribute property and violate rights based on "need." He knew that once the camel got its nose under the tent it would eventually get all the way in.

But most conservatives pay no heed to Mr. Madison or the other Founders these days.

Another example is the stance that Davy Crockett took on the floor of the Senate when the question of public charity came up. A contemporary of

Crockett's, Edward S. Ellis, relates the following story in his 1884 book, *The Life of Colonel David Crockett…*

> I was one day in the lobby of the House of Representatives when a bill was taken up appropriating money for the benefit of a widow of a distinguished naval officer. Several beautiful speeches had been made in its support – rather, as I thought, because it afforded the speakers a fine opportunity for display than from the necessity of convincing anybody, for it seemed to me that everybody favored it. The Speaker was just about to put the question when Crockett arose. Everybody expected, of course, that he was going to make one of his characteristic speeches in support of the bill. He commenced:
>
> "Mr. Speaker – I have as much respect for the memory of the deceased, and as much sympathy for the sufferings of the living, if suffering there be, as any man in this House, but we must not permit our respect for the dead or our sympathy for a part of the living to lead us into an act of injustice to the balance of the living. I will not go into an argument to prove that Congress has no power to appropriate this money as an act of charity. Every member upon this floor knows it. We have the right, as individuals, to give away as much of our own money as we please in charity; but as members of Congress we have no right so to appropriate a dollar of the public money. Some eloquent appeals have been made to us upon the ground that it is a debt due the deceased. Mr. Speaker, the deceased lived long after the close of the war; he was in office to the day of his death, and I have never heard that the government was in arrears to him. This government can owe no debts but for services rendered, and at a stipulated price. If it is a debt, how much is it? Has it been audited, and the amount due ascertained? If it is a debt, this is not the place to present it for payment, or to have its merits examined. If it is a debt, we owe more than we can ever hope to pay, for we owe the widow of every soldier who fought in the War of 1812 precisely the same amount. There is a woman in my neighborhood, the widow of as gallant a man as ever shouldered a musket. He fell in battle.
>
> She is as good in every respect as this lady, and is as poor. She is earning her daily bread by her daily labor; but if I were to introduce a bill to appropriate five or ten thousand dollars for her benefit, I should be laughed at, and my bill would not get five votes in this House. There are thousands of widows in the country just such as the one I have spoken of, but we never hear of any of these large debts to them. Sir, this is no debt. The government did not owe it to the deceased when he was alive; it could not contract it after he died. I do not wish to be rude, but I must be plain.
>
> Every man in this House knows it is not a debt. We cannot, without the grossest corruption, appropriate this money as the payment of a debt. We have not the semblance of authority to appropriate it as a charity. Mr. Speaker, I have said we have the right to give as much of our own money as we please. I am the poorest man on this floor. I cannot vote for this bill, but I will give one week's pay to the object, and if every member of Congress will do the same, it will amount to more than the bill asks."

He took his seat. Nobody replied. The bill was put upon its passage, and, instead of passing unanimously, as was generally supposed, and as, no doubt, it would, but for that speech, it received but few votes, and, of course, was lost.

Ellis and several other members of Congress were furious at Crockett for this. When Ellis later questioned him about it, Crockett told him a story about a previous encounter with one of his constituents, a backwoods farmer. The Farmer had told Crockett he would not vote for him again because he had previously voted to appropriate $20,000 for public charity. As the farmer explained it…

> It is not the amount, Colonel, that I complain of; it is the principle. In the first place, the government ought to have in the Treasury no more than enough for its legitimate purposes. But that has nothing to do with the question. The power of collecting and disbursing money at pleasure is the most dangerous power that can be entrusted to man, particularly under our system of collecting revenue by a tariff, which reaches every man in the country, no matter how poor he may be, and the poorer he is the more he pays in proportion to his means. What is worse, it presses upon him without his knowledge where the weight centers, for there is not a man in the United States who can ever guess how much he pays to the government. So you see, that while you are contributing to relieve one, you are drawing it from thousands who are even worse off than he. If you had the right to give anything, the amount was simply a matter of discretion with you, and you had as much right to give $20,000,000 as $20,000. If you have the right to give to one, you have the right to give to all; and, as the Constitution neither defines charity nor stipulates the amount, you are at liberty to give to any and everything which you may believe, or profess to believe, is a charity, and to any amount you may think proper. You will very easily perceive what a wide door this would open for fraud and corruption and favoritism, on the one hand, and for robbing the people on the other. No, Colonel, Congress has no right to give charity. Individual members may give as much of their own money as they please, but they have no right to touch a dollar of the public money for that purpose.

This story illustrates the point clearly: it is the principle that matters. Had we upheld the Constitution and our original principles, we would not be in the mess we are in today—a country heading toward destruction and bankruptcy because of a government that has virtually no limitations on it.

I guess the present trends are not surprising, when you consider that Congress was once filled with people like James Madison and David Crockett… and now it's populated by the likes of Nancy Pelosi and Barney Frank.

If liberals and conservatives were truly compassionate, if they truly cared about the advancement and well-being of all Americans, then they would uphold the Constitution and support the one social system that has resulted in unparalleled human progress and advancement: Capitalism.

But today's conservatives run from capitalism because capitalism upholds individual liberty and a man's right to work for his own gain and profit. Capitalism upholds the right of the individual to purse his own happiness and that of his family—with apologies to no one. Capitalism also requires a strictly limited government and a separation of economics and state as well as a separation of religion and state.

Conservatives are squeamish about true freedom and laissez faire capitalism because (a) they believe in original sin and the depravity of man (therefore, they believe, if left truly free, men will exploit and harm others); (b) a little voice is always in their heads asking them "what would Jesus do?"; and (c) it reduces their power and importance as politicians.

Conservatives believe deep down in the ethics of self-sacrifice—altruism has been drilled into their heads by the pulpit and their parents since they were very young—so they quake in fear when a liberal brands them with two little words: "you're selfish." Those two words used on a conservative politician have the same effect that kryptonite has on Superman.

When people call others selfish, they are really saying "you are doing something I don't want you to do." It's not just six year olds that have a hidden agenda when they use the term. The adult response to being called selfish by a liberal do-gooder who wants the government to redistribute your income is to say "Too bad, I'll decide what to do with my own money and time. If I'm going to donate it to charities, I'll decide that and I'll pick them myself. Go mind your own business."

Although compassionate conservatism was the leitmotif of George W. Bush, Neo-conservatism has probably been even more of an influence on the modern conservative movement.

Neoconservatives

The neoconservatives are the more intellectual faction of the postwar conservatives. They run the conservative think-tanks, manage the leading conservative journals and magazines, and many teach in universities.

One of the neoconservatives' most prominent intellectual spokesmen, David Brooks, of The New York Times said, "we're all neoconservatives now." Given the fact that the old right, the Goldwater right, is long gone, Brooks has a point. So "who are these guys" and what are they trying to accomplish?

The first thing you should know is that neo-conservatism had its origins among disillusioned liberal intellectuals during the 1970's. Many of them were former Trotskyites and Marxists.

The second thing you need to know is that the neocons count "among their heroes," Theodore Roosevelt and Franklin Delano Roosevelt. Those two facts tell you all you need to know right there. However, let's look a little closer at what neoconservatives are all about.

Irving Kristol, the "godfather" of neo-conservatism (and father of Weekly Standard editor Bill Kristol) give us a clue. He says their goal is to "convert the Republican party, and American conservatism in general, against their respective wills, into a new kind of conservative politics suitable to governing a modern democracy." And how does he define a "modern democracy." It's clear that he means a very big government.

Kristol goes on....

> But they [neocons] are impatient with the Hayekian notion that we are on "the road to serfdom." Neocons do not feel that kind of alarm or anxiety about the growth of the state in the past century, seeing it as natural, indeed inevitable.

Natural and inevitable? So these so-called defenders of American tradition have already thrown in the towel. The only question that matters to neoconservatives is "whose gang is going to rule" and preside over a powerful and omnipotent government.

So when the neocons are in charge there are some minor policy differences. For example, taxpayer dollars are redirected from public welfare agencies to "faith-based" organizations, but the net effect is the same: the property of some Americans is taken by force and redistributed for "compassionate" purposes.

Just Plain Cons

Conservatives have been "conning" us by pretending they stand for Liberty. The vast majority do not.

At bottom, the original credo of most conservatives is not the one outlined by the Founding Fathers, it was the one laid out by their Pilgrim forefathers. The character traits that the "compassionate conservatives" and "neo-conservatives" want to establish echo the ones that the Puritans regarded as virtuous—the religious ones. Religion teaches the slave-virtues: obedience to authority; humility; self-denial; self-sacrifice; submission; unconditional forgiveness; non-resistance.

As Robert Ingersoll put it...

> Lips, religious and fearful, tremblingly repeat this passage: "Though he slay me, yet will I trust him." This is the abyss of degradation. Religion does not teach self-reliance, independence, manliness, courage, self-defense. Religion makes God a master and man his serf. The master cannot be great enough to make slavery sweet.

The sad fact of the matter is, the underlying ideas that generate most conservative policies are the ones found in Jefferson's Bible, not the ones contained in his philosophy of Government. That is not a basis for a country founded on Liberty.

Conservatism and The Vortex Of Need

Like liberals, conservatives believe we have a duty to serve those in need. But they never ask the next logical question: if we have a duty to serve those in need (via forced government redistribution), then where does it stop? Under conservatives, it doesn't, because they have no moral defense for freedom and self-interest.

The poor need our help? Take it. People that choose not to buy Health Insurance need our help? Take it. People that can't afford to buy homes need our help? Take it. Farmers need our help? Take it. People in Africa need our help? The Palestinians need our help? Take it.

AIG needs our help? Take it. Bear Stearns needs our help? Take it. Citigroup needs our help? Take it. GM and Chrysler need our help? Take it.

This is where accepting a "duty" based on the needs of others leads. There is no end to the "needs" of others. Need is always and everywhere present. Accepting the premise that the needs of some constitute a political claim on the life and property of others leads to economic and cultural suicide.

The American government is now bankrupt due to all of this so-called "compassion." The national debt is now more than $15 trillion and counting — and when you include unfunded liabilities for Social Security and Medicare the true number is closer to $100 trillion. That amounts to a debt of more than $1 million per American household! Eventually someone is going to have to pay the piper.

The grotesque fact is it won't be us—the ones who have made (or been complicit in making) this mess—it will be our children. We are throwing away our children's futures based on this nonsense and corruption. Whether it's out of liberal pity, misplaced guilt, Christian love, Comtean altruism, the power lust of politicians, misguided policy, or sheer stupidity, it matters not… the welfare state expands and expands… growing every year and adding new recipients and victims all the time.

Where does it end? We know where it ends. Look at the history of the 20th Century. Look at Soviet Russia and Nazi Germany. Look at Argentina and Cuba. Look at what is happening in Greece, Ireland, the UK and all across Europe as I write this.

Wake up American Conservatives!

Now, having lambasted conservatives, let me say a word in their defense: they don't really mean to do it. Unlike liberals, I believe that most conservatives do love America and don't really want to "remake" it as a European socialist state. The trouble is, conservatives don't understand the un-resolvable contradiction between religion and America.

When it comes right down it, accepting an irrational set of beliefs, based on the unproven assertions of other men and an old series of books written by primitives is not conducive to Liberty or Freedom.

Most of those men whose words conservatives place such stock in (preachers and priests) have an agenda. Remember that, like politicians, the clergy produce nothing of their own and live off alms. "All beggars teach that others should give," said Ingersoll.

And all of this irrationality is held together by an ethics that is even worse — the primitive morality of human sacrifice.

America is based on the pursuit of happiness, which comes from pursuing reason, self-interest and productive achievement. In other words, it is the opposite of Christianity.

Here is the fact that honest Christians must face if they truly care about preserving this Republic: your barbarian Bible and its primitive creed is un-American! It is undermining the foundations of our country and it always has.

There was a time when the Republican party did stand for reason and liberty. There was a time when it was not infested with Satan-fearing religionists, calculating and corrupt politicians and former Trotskyites. For example, the original Republican Party of Lincoln was not a product of the religious right. In fact, Lincoln himself was not a serious Christian, he was very much a freethinker. The original Republican party was the party of the future, of the advancement and liberation of mankind. People forget that it was the Republican party that ended the scourge of slavery; it was the Democrat party that undermined liberation at every turn.

A truly free society must be based on Reason. It simply cannot be preserved on the shifting quicksand and subjectivism of religious faith—any religious faith.

Christians have gone to great lengths to try to spin the Bible and Christianity's ethics as somehow being pro-American and pro-Capitalism. But no matter how much pretzel logic is used, you will never get around this one irrefragable fact: your ideal man ended up hanging dead on a cross in a human sacrifice supposedly to "take away the sins of the world." His Father, supposedly possessing omnipotence—and therefore the power to save him—let him suffer hideously and die, even though he was innocent.

That's some "ideal" there.

Religionists will say that was done to teach a lesson. Yes, and what is the lesson? That we should sacrifice the good because it is good. We are still paying the price of such a perverse moral lesson today, and our country suffers greatly for it. Due to their underlying altruist-collectivist ethics, conservatives are ideologically unarmed. They can talk a good game, but underneath it all they accept all the premises of their avowed liberal enemies due to a shared ethics. Jesus and Karl are two peas in a pod. And that is the primary reason why conservatives have expanded the Leviathan state and delivered us straight into the hands of our anti-Liberty enemies.

Republicans are in intellectual confusion due to contradictory ideals and have thus been unable to provide any principled opposition to the socialist juggernaut. We are like a mouse caught between the right and left paws of a big cat… just being tossed back and forth while deluding ourselves there is a difference between each side.

Does that mean the alternative is the Libertarian party? Unfortunately, no, not by a long shot. Despite their name, the Libertarian party is more anti-government than they are pro-Liberty. Historically, they count many anarchists among their intellectual influences and often tolerate (or even glorify) anarchism. Many of their most prominent leaders, such as Ron Paul, blame America for the Islamist assaults against us and their foreign policy is naïve at best and dangerous at worst. They also embrace an "anything goes" moral subjectivism and offer no coherent theory as to what constitutes freedom or force. Although libertarian scholars have made huge contributions in economics, the Libertarian party itself is an inconsistent defender of the American Ideal of Liberty.

A Rational Alternative

So if our present road to serfdom has been paved by both liberals and conservatives, by an unholy alliance of religion and socialism, what do we do? What chance do we have? Is there a rational alternative to all of this?

Fortunately for us, there is. Because in 1926, while our "progressive" socialists were slashing and burning our Constitution and stomping on the Declaration of Independence… while the American government was consolidating control of business and manipulating the country into a speculative bubble that was about to burst... while the Bolsheviks were burning down Alexandria and a young Adolf Hitler was making speeches in German beer halls… while Mussolini was seizing control in Italy and

Hirohito in Japan… a boat carrying a diminutive woman, who was escaping from Russia, landed at Ellis Island.

America was about to get her greatest defender….

CHAPTER 11

A PHILOSOPHY WORTHY OF AMERICA

There are a thousand hacking at the branches of evil, to one who is striking at the root. —Henry David Thoreau

If we are going to save this country from a Statist future, we have got to get beyond Jesus and Marx. We just have to. If we continue this irrational worship of the god of the sky and/or the god of the state—and their corresponding altruist-collectivist ethics—this country is doomed. This is especially true when you consider we are being assaulted on two fronts: statism internally and Islam externally.

Despite their eminence, despite their monumental achievements, the Founding Fathers were not able to formulate a consistent and non-contradictory theory of morality and rights to undergird their brilliant political theory and architecture of government. I believe that was far more than we could have asked of them, given the context of their times. Besides, they had a lot on their plate.

What they did in winning the revolution and advancing the first political system based on liberty in human history was heroic and unparalleled. However, we should not make the mistake that many conservatives do and pretend they were "gods," whose pronouncements came out fully perfected like the myth of Moses on Sinai. To do so is to demean and diminish the incredible achievements of the real, flesh and blood humans they were. Although their achievements were immense, there were contradictions in their philosophies and cracks in their political system.

Their work was incomplete.

Fortunately for us, here in the land of the individual, one individual has completed their work by developing a comprehensive philosophy that honors them and is worthy of the American Ideal.

Her name was Ayn Rand and her philosophy is called Objectivism. If you're familiar with Rand, then you already know that this book has been heavily influenced by her ideas. In fact, what I have been offering throughout the book is essentially her defense of the American Ideal of Liberty and I freely admit that. Ayn Rand's accomplishments were immense. By having the courage and integrity to follow the dictates of her own reason, she challenged 2000 years of philosophy and conventional thinking.

Her critics say that most of her ideas are not new or revolutionary and that's true to a degree. She was not the first to advocate reason in epistemology or declare that happiness and self-interest were virtues for example. She was not the first to challenge religion.

However, she was the first to provide a full and complete moral justification for capitalism and individualism by showing—in no uncertain terms—the evils of altruism and the nobility of individualism and egoism. She was also the first to demonstrate why Liberty must rest squarely on a foundation of Reason and an ethic of rational self-interest or it cannot be properly defended.

Most of all, she completed the political revolution of the Founding Fathers by providing a moral foundation for the individuals' right to life, liberty and the pursuit of happiness.

When first encountering Rand, many people (including this writer), are amazed to find out that the author of *The Fountainhead* and *Atlas Shrugged* was a woman and a Russian immigrant. Why? Because women did not write about businessmen and entrepreneurs, and her understanding of America and American history had such incredible depth, it seems impossible that anyone but a native-born American could write like that.

But Miss Rand was truly a unique individual....

"When They Ask You in America, Tell Them Russia Is a Huge Cemetery And We Are All Dying."

Ayn Rand was born Alissa Rosenbaum on February 2, 1905 in St. Petersburg, Russia. She taught herself to read at the age of six and by the age of nine she knew she wanted to be a writer. In high school, she was an eyewitness to the Bolshevik Revolution of 1917, which she denounced.

One night the Bolsheviks stormed her father's pharmacy and declared it the property of the government. To escape the fighting, her family moved from St. Petersburg to the Crimea where she finished High School. She was introduced to American history in her final year of high school and immediately recognized America as the model of what a nation of free men could be.

Her family returned from the Crimea in 1920 and she entered the University of Petrograd to study philosophy and history. There she witnessed the takeover of the university by communist thugs. Since she understood the Communist threat—and knew where it would lead—she was determined to escape Russia. In 1926, she obtained permission to leave for a short-term visit to relatives in the United States. Before she left, a cousin said to her, "When they ask you in America, tell them Russia is a huge cemetery and we are all dying." Rand knew she would never return to Russia.

Those of us who were born in America can only imagine the feelings that she, and millions of other immigrants, experienced when sailing into New York Harbor for the first time, seeing the lights or the skyline of New York. For a young, aspiring writer like Ayn Rand, it must have been overwhelming. To her, New York was the center of the universe—the greatest city in the shining country that was the beacon and the engine of the world.

Her boat docked on a cold, February night in 1926. As Rand's words explain in the film *Ayn Rand: A Sense of Life*, "It was dark then. It was kind of early evening, I think about seven o'clock or so. And seeing the first lighted skyscrapers — it was snowing very faintly, and I think I began to cry because I remember feeling the snowflakes and the tears sort of together."

She lived in America for the rest of her life, until her death in 1982. In the United States, she changed her name to Ayn Rand, most likely to protect her family who was still living in Russia under Stalin. After moving to Hollywood shortly after arriving in America, she worked briefly as an extra at Cecil B. DeMille's studios and then struggled for years as a screenwriter, working on screen plays and short stories.

During this period she also wrote her first novel, *We The Living*, and the novella, *Anthem*. *We The Living*, which is her semi-autobiographical story of a young woman living in Communist Russia, was eventually published in 1936. It showed what the socialist theory means in practice, amid the backdrop of Soviet Russia.

Anthem was published in 1938 in England, but was not published in the U.S. until 1946 (largely due to opposition by collectivist intellectuals in the 1930's). *Anthem* is a story about what happens to a young and independent-thinking person in a totalitarian state, where freedom of thought and expression have been abolished. The word "I" has been banned from the language—it has become the one unmentionable word—and everyone must only say "we." Perhaps the reason it was difficult to publish was because it hit a little too close to home in FDR's America.

When she was living in Russia, Rand saw America as her greatest hope as did millions of others in oppressive countries. America has always been the place where people could escape to. From the beginning of our history, America has offered a refuge for those seeking freedom from tyrants big and small. However, America has increasingly begun to resemble some of those places that people were fleeing from. After her arrival in America it didn't take Ayn Rand long to realize this.

In the late 1930's, she began working on her first major book, *The Fountainhead*. In this story about the architect Howard Roark, she dramatized the role of the individual vs. the state. After being turned down by twelve publishers, with most of them citing that it was too intellectual for commercial success, *The Fountainhead* was published in 1943 by Bobbs-Merrill and established her literary reputation. It went on to sell 6.5 million copies and continues to sell well over 100,000 copies per year. The character of Roark is unforgettable and the book stands as the best tribute to individualism ever written.

The character of Howard Roark exemplifies what Rand considered the cardinal virtues: rationality, integrity, independence, honesty, justice, productivity, purpose, pride and self-esteem. Through the character of Roark she demonstrates why those are the highest virtues of the human spirit. It is this creative human spirit, a combination of reason and passion, that has lifted man out of the dark ages.

> Thousands of years ago the first man discovered how to make fire. He was probably burned at the stake he had taught his brothers to light, but he left them a gift they had not conceived of, and he lifted darkness off the earth. Throughout the centuries there were men who took first steps down new roads, armed with nothing but their own vision. The great creators, the thinkers, the artists, the scientists, the inventors, stood alone against the men of their time. Every new thought was opposed. Every new invention was denounced. But the men of unborrowed vision went ahead. They fought, they suffered, and they paid — but they won.
>
> — Howard Roark in *The Fountainhead*

Had she only written *The Fountainhead*, she would have secured her place in literary history. However, she followed that with an even more ambitious novel that has become one of the most popular books of all time.

Atlas Shrugged

In 1946, Rand began work on her greatest novel, *Atlas Shrugged*. Atlas was published in 1957 and stands as Rand's magnum opus. It took her a decade to write it and she claimed that she wrote every page of the 1,000 page book a minimum of five times. The results speak for themselves. In a Library of Congress survey, it was cited as the second most influential book of all time (the first was the Bible unfortunately).

Ayn Rand held a profound respect for the American Ideal of 1776. Like Jefferson, she shared the hope that America would serve as a model for the rest of the world. In her 1974 address to the graduates of West Point, she said the following:

> The United States of America is the greatest, the noblest, and in its original founding principles, the only moral country in the history of the world.

In a way, John Galt, Francisco D'Anconia, Ragnar Danneskjold, and the other heroes in the book can be seen as Patriot leaders of a second American Revolution.

The premise of *Atlas Shrugged* is this: what would happen to the world if its greatest thinkers and producers—its entrepreneurs, scientists, philosophers, inventors, industrialists, and artists—went on strike? What would happen if those who produce everything decided they have "had it" with those who produce nothing, yet seek to control and live off the labors and efforts of the productive?

Her answer was that America would collapse. And remember, she was writing and predicting this long before the collapse of the Soviet Union. Much has been made of her prescience in predicting the events that are unfolding before our very eyes today in America. Rand would say that she was not a prophet, simply someone who understood that man is governed by ideas, and ideas have consequences.

In *Atlas Shrugged*, she painstakingly dramatized the role of man's mind in society and demonstrated what happens when force is used to try to control and thwart the freedom of thought and action. *Atlas Shrugged* is Rand's moral defense of freedom, based on several related points: (a) that an individual has the right to his own life: (b) that he furthers his life through the use of his reason; (c) that a man's right to think and live for himself requires a system of political and economic freedom (capitalism).

Before the book was published, one of the editors at Random House, Donald Klopfer, recognized that her uniquely secular moral defense of capitalism was in opposition to 2000 years of Judeo-Christian tradition and said so at the time. Rand praised him for his perceptiveness and said he was exactly right but it didn't frighten her in the least. To their credit, it didn't frighten Klopfer or Random House either and they published it in 1957, knowing it would be highly controversial.

The reviews at the time were generally scathing from both the right and the left sides of the political spectrum. It was panned mercilessly by both liberal and conservative reviewers. How could that be, considering it is now one of the most popular books of all time? The reason it was panned by intellectuals on both the left and right when it came out, is because Atlas is a well-sharpened ax striking at the root and shaking the tree that those on the left and the right share—the tree of altruism and collectivism—and they knew it.

Or to put it another way, it was the intellectual equivalent of Henry Knox's guns, poised high on a hill and pointed at both the religionists and the socialists, who were trapped below in the valley of their own contradictions.

To see what they were so afraid of, let's look at a few examples from Galt's speech in Atlas in sections that focus on faith and religion. Whereas Ingersoll before her also attacked religion, he did it in a more positive way with great personal charm and humor. In Ingersoll's day he could afford to be magnanimous because he was convinced that religion was dying of its own primitive weight and would soon yield to the light of reason, progress and science.

However, by 1957, Rand could see that was not the case. She could see that it was not just the superstition and irrationality of religion that was a problem—it was the underlying morality that needed to be exposed as evil. Where Ingersoll appealed to reason and progress, Rand goes right for the jugular with a greater sense of urgency.

From Galt's speech…

> Through centuries of scourges and disasters, brought about by your code of morality, you have cried that your code had been broken, that the scourges were punishment for breaking it, that men were too weak and too selfish to spill all the blood it required. You damned man, you damned existence, you damned this earth, but never dared to question your code. Your victims took the blame and struggled on with your curses as reward for their martyrdom – while you went on crying that your code was noble but human nature was not good enough to practice it. And no one rose to ask the question: Good? By what standard? You wanted to know John Galt's identity. I am the man who asked that question.

She is talking about the Christian code of self-sacrifice, the essence of altruism. Such a code can only be perpetrated on a people when they don't truly value themselves and their own lives. That's why this Christian code begins with the idea of an original sin and the damnation of man and this world, while the "spiritual" world is held up as the good. Rand sees the evil in that as well as in the idea that any positive moral code can come from such a concept.

She has Galt go on:

> Yes, this is an age of moral crisis. Yes, you are bearing punishment for your evil. But it is not man who is now on trial and it is not human na-ture that will take the blame. It is your moral code that's through this time. Your moral code has reached its climax, the blind alley at the end of its course. And if you wish to go on living, what you need is not to return to morality—you who have never known any—but to discover it.

This is the link that was missing from the Founder's vision. Their radical political vision, which upheld the liberty of the individual, was mired in the muck of Judeo-Christian morality and its concept of self-sacrifice. That is an unresolvable contradiction and, sooner or later, the more powerful force will win out. Morality is more powerful than politics.

Rand fully understood this:

> For centuries, the battle of morality was fought between those who claimed that your life belongs to God and those who claimed that it belongs to your neighbors – between those who preached that the good is self-sacrifice for the sake of ghosts in heaven and those who preached that the good is self-sacrifice for the sake of incompetents on earth. And no one came to say that your life belongs to you and the good is to live it.

Rand understood that a code of morality that is forced on you, or that is done out of blind obedience and fear, is no code of morality at all. She understood that morality was the province of reason, not faith or force, and that it depends on choice and free will. Later in the speech Galt says…

> A code of values accepted by choice is a code of morality. Whoever you are, you who are hearing me now, I am speaking to whatever living remnant is left uncorrupted in you, to the remnant of the human, to your mind, and I say: There is a morality of reason, a morality proper to man, and Man's Life is its standard of value. All that which is proper to the life of a rational being is the good; all that destroys it is the evil. … The purpose of morality is to teach you, not to suffer and die, but to enjoy yourself and live.

Rand's concept of a rational morality, with man's life on earth as its standard of value, is consistent with the American ideal of "life, liberty and the pursuit of happiness." The Christian idea of morality, with its emphasis on self-sacrifice, placing others above yourself, and the denigration of this life in favor of "a better life" after we die, is the opposite of the American ideal of Liberty.

She also demonstrates the link between faith and force, explains that rational men deal with each other peacefully, as traders exchanging values, and then takes to task all of those who would force their opinions on others at the point of a gun…

> Whatever may be open to disagreement, there is one act of evil that may not, the act that no man may commit against others and no man may sanction or forgive. So long as men desire to live together, no man may initiate – do you hear me? – no man may start – the

> use of physical force against others. Do not open your mouth to tell me that your mind has convinced you of your right to force my mind. Force and mind are opposites. Morality ends where a gun begins.

She equates religion with a worship of the zero, a worship of nothing. She contrasts those who tear down with those who build.

> You who are worshippers of the zero – you have never discovered that achieving life is not the same as avoiding death. You seek escape from pain. We seek the achievement of happiness. You exist for the sake of avoiding punishment. We exist for the sake of earning rewards. Threats will not make us function; fear is not our incentive. It is not death we wish to avoid, but life that we wish to live.

She then demolishes the foundation of Christianity and demonstrates the perverse nature of the concept of Original Sin in a single paragraph:

> Damnation is the start of your morality, destruction is its purpose, means and end. Your code begins by damning man as evil, then demands that he practice a good which it defines as impossible for him to practice. It demands, as his first proof of virtue, that he accept his own depravity without proof. It demands that he start, not with a standard of value, but with a standard of evil, which is himself, by means of which he is then to define the good: the good is that which he is not.

As the speech goes on, she continues to demonstrate how the morality of sacrifice is shared by those on both the left and the right. Socialism is simply a secularized version of Christianity as we discussed in previous chapters. The common thread is the morality of sacrifice and an abandonment of reason:

> Under a morality of sacrifice, the first value you sacrifice is morality; the next is self-esteem. When need is the standard, every man is both a victim and a parasite. As a victim, he must labor to fill the needs of others, leaving himself in the position of a parasite whose needs must be filled by others. He cannot approach his fellow men except in one of two disgraceful roles: he is both a beggar and a sucker.

Is this not the religio-socialist morass we find ourselves in today?

Rand called the autocrats of the left the "mystics of muscle" and the autocrats of the right the "mystics of spirit."

> The mystics of spirit curse matter, the mystics of muscle curse profit. The first wish men to profit by renouncing the earth, the second wish men to inherit the earth by renouncing all profit. Their non-material, non-profit worlds are realms where rivers run with milk and coffee, where wine spurts from rocks at their command, where pastry drops on them from clouds at the price of opening their mouth. On this material, profit-chasing earth, an enormous investment of virtue – of intelligence, integrity, energy, skill – is required to construct a railroad to carry them the distance of one mile; in their non-material, non-profit world, they travel from planet to planet at the cost of a wish. If an honest person asks them how? They answer with righteous scorn that a "how" is the concept of vulgar realists; the concept of superior spirits is "Somehow."

Yes, just like we will "somehow" add thirty million people to the health care system and it will actually save money and improve the quality of care. If you just wish upon a star.

Despite the fear it induced in the intellectuals of the time, *Atlas* has been embraced by the American people at large. In fact, it founded a movement and now, some 50+ years later, it is also gaining a growing number of intellectual supporters in the universities and academia.

In the Tea Party rallies of recent years, there are always signs and speeches referencing *Atlas Shrugged*, showing the book has helped spur this movement. Sales have been increasing for decades to a level never seen in Ayn Rand's lifetime. In fact, in 2009, sales of *Atlas Shrugged* hit 500,000 copies, a new sales record and more than double the amount of sales in 2008. Sales of the book have tripled since President Obama took office. This explosion in sales of *Atlas Shrugged* more than a half century after its initial publication is remarkable.

Why now? Because people are looking for answers and discovering the prescience of her writing. They're seeing the policies of the book's villains such as Wesley Mouch and Cuffy Meigs acted out by our government officials today.

In *Atlas*, she did a masterful job of showing how raw political power—which she called "the aristocracy of pull"—replaces the free market and voluntary exchange as the means of deciding who gets what. Once that happens, the downward spiral begins. Everyone seeks to live at the expense of everyone else. Government agents begin to micro-manage and regulate private companies to make sure they have control and can pick winners and losers based on their preferences.

In *Atlas*, Cuffy Meigs is the politician who pulls the strings at Taggart Transcontinental in order to get favors for his cronies. The Obama administration plays the same game by putting bureaucrats and political friends on the boards of auto companies and banks that it has bailed out or taken over. In Atlas, Wesley Mouch was the economic dictator of the "Bureau of Economic Planning and Natural Resources." Under the Obama administration we now have more than 30 unelected "czars," some of which have been avowed Communists, and none of whom were even approved by Congress.

And then we have people like Rep. Barney Frank (D-MA), who was one of the principals in facilitating Fannie Mae's "affordable housing" policies which resulted in all the bad loans that triggered the 2008 financial crisis. Just months before the banks crashed, Representative Frank was pressuring Fannie to liberalize lending policies for the purchase of condominiums. Later, once Fannie and all of the other banks holding bad loans collapsed, Frank hauled bank executives before congressional committees where he denounced them for their "greed" and spewed and spit like a bully threatening them with punitive government action. I don't think even Ayn Rand could have dreamt up such a character.

In contrast to villains like Mouch in the book and Frank in Congress, the heroes of the book are the producers—the most able, intelligent, hardest-working members of society. These include the over-achievers like John Galt, Hank Rearden and Dagny Taggart, as well as a cast of honest, hard-working characters throughout the book. What is common among all the heroes is that they never seek the unearned—they have no desire to live parasitically off others nor do they have any desire to rule over or control others. They do desire to be left alone to pursue their own happiness and achieve their own goals and values. Likewise, they do not expect others to live parasitically off them. Their oath is, "I swear by my life and my love of it that I will never live for the sake of another man, nor ask another man to live for mine."

Throughout the book, Rand contrasts the differences between the productive class of creators, and the parasitical class of destroyers. The creators and producers operate economically (in freedom); the destroyers and parasites operate politically (through force). She shows what happens when politicians come to believe their own lies. They become so irrationally devoted to power at all costs they evade objective reality. You can see this throughout the book.

In a scene toward the end of the book, the bureaucratic dictators explain to Hank Rearden, the steel magnate, that they intend to "save" his industry (i.e., his incompetent competition), through something called a "Steel Unification Plan." The Steel Unification Plan, they explain, will take all of the income from steel producers and place it into a common pool that will be distributed to manufacturers based on how many furnaces each owns. An incredulous Rearden explains the math to them:

> Orren Boyle's Associated Steel owns 60 open-hearth furnaces, one-third of them standing idle and the rest producing an average of 300 tons of steel per day. I own 20 open-hearth furnaces working at capacity, producing 750 tons of Rearden Metal per furnace per day. So we own "pooled" furnaces with a "pooled" output of 27,000 tons, which makes an

average of 337.5 tons per furnace. Each day of the year, I produce 15,000 tons, will be paid for 6,750 tons. Boyle, producing 12,000 tones, will be paid for 20,250 tons. Now how long do you expect me to last under your plan?

Rearden can't believe that these supposedly grown men are actually suggesting such nonsense. Their only answers to him are, "In times of national peril, it's your duty to serve." And "you must make sacrifices to the public welfare," And "you'll manage."

Similar math is being used by politicians in the real world today as they say, with straight faces, that adding thirty million people to the health care system, dictating to doctors and insurance companies, and establishing a vast government bureaucracy to manage it all, will somehow "save" the public money. This, despite the fact that a similar government program, Medicare, wound up costing fifteen times more than the government's projections at the time (and the same with every government program that's ever been enacted). Drunk with power and blinded by their desire to force their ideas on others, they evade reality themselves and play us all for fools.

It is through this process of evasion that we find ourselves in our present circumstances. Rand shows not only how politicians spin facts to suit their agenda, but the extent to which they believe their own lies and systematically engage in evading reality. And it is not just politicians that engage in it. A large percentage of the population does the same thing.

You might point out to a politician that we are already $15 trillion in debt with unfunded liabilities mounting to around $100 trillion. Their answer, "we need to spend more!" You might ask, "what about our children and grandchildren, whose backs you're placing all of this debt on? Their answer? "The hell with them, I'm up for election in November!"

Or take the "Global Warming" issue. You can point out that the earth has not been warming for almost a decade and that since the "Climategate" fraud was exposed in 2010, it's blatantly apparent that the man-made global warming data is garbage and the whole thing was driven by politics, not science. Their answer? But we need a "cap and trade" scheme in order to save the planet! No matter that it will cost trillions of dollars, double our electric bills, destroy jobs, and generally retard industrial progress. All for nothing.

That's ok, we'll all "manage."

Atlas is achieving such popularity today because it showed the logical consequences of following altruist-collectivist ideas and systematically evading reality. Unfortunately, despite Rand's warnings, we have followed that road and we are now dealing with those consequences.

At bottom, Atlas shows why it's necessary to truly embrace reason and liberty in order to stop this slide toward tyranny. She demonstrates how even small compromises on principle lead to disaster. She shows not only how politicians spin facts to suit their agenda, but the extent to which they will pursue their agendas even when their policies are economic suicide. Collectivist economic experiments have already been tried and everyone knows they end in disaster, yet here we go again.

Why? It's because, although we learned the economic lessons, we never learned the moral lessons. Politicians are still able to appeal to the morality of altruism to enact their economy and liberty killing agendas. Conservatives, even when speaking against Obamacare, will still say things like, "although it's noble for the President to want to insure 30 million Americans, we don't think we can afford it." That is a losing argument. It is not noble because noble ends cannot be achieved through ignoble means (force and theft). By taking that approach, Conservatives cede the moral high ground to their alleged enemies. That is a deadly mistake.

Taking The Torch From The Founders

Rand's major achievement in Atlas, as well as in her philosophy of Objectivism, was the moral defense of freedom. Where the Founding Fathers provided the political framework for freedom, it was doomed to fail without the proper moral defense of liberty.

Ayn Rand provides that…

> My philosophy, in essence, is the concept of man as a heroic being. With happiness is his highest goal, productive achievement as his noblest activity, and reason as his only absolute. — Ayn Rand

Obviously, a full explanation of Rand's philosophy is outside the scope of our discussion, but I would like to briefly touch on the key elements that support the American Ideal of Liberty.

First, we need to remember that Politics is only one branch of Philosophy. As Rand points out in many of her writings, Politics is really applying moral principles to society.

The answers given by ethics determine how man should treat other men, and this determines the fourth branch of philosophy: politics, which defines the principles of a proper social system. As an example of philosophy's function, political philosophy will not tell you how much rationed gas you should be given and on which day of the week—it will tell you whether the government has the right to impose any rationing on anything.

In the previous chapters we discussed how the American Ideal of the individual's right to life, liberty and the pursuit of happiness is incompatible with religious and socialist ideals. The religio-socialist ideals are in fact in direct conflict with the individual's pursuit of his own happiness.

Rand pulled no punches and had an incredible gift for cutting through the fog and the B.S. Here she is on the proper purpose of government:

> The only proper purpose of a government is to protect man's rights, which means: to protect him from physical violence. A proper government is only a policeman, acting as an agent of man's self-defense, and, as such, may resort to force only against those who start the use of force. The only proper functions of a government are: the police, to protect you from criminals; the army, to protect you from foreign invaders; and the courts, to protect your property and contracts from breach or fraud by others, to settle disputes by rational rules, according to objective law. But a government that initiates the employment of force against men who had forced no one, the employment of armed compulsion against disarmed victims, is a nightmare infernal machine designed to annihilate morality: such a government reverses its only moral purpose and switches from the role of protector to the role of man's deadliest enemy, from the role of policeman to the role of a criminal vested with the right to the wielding of violence against victims deprived of the right of self-defense. Such a government substitutes for morality the following rule of social conduct: you may do whatever you please to your neighbor, provided your gang is bigger than his.
> — "This is John Galt Speaking," For the New Intellectual

Ayn Rand called Objectivism, "a philosophy for living on earth," because it is a moral philosophy that is consistent with man's nature and upholds the right of the individual to rationally pursue his own self-interest and seek happiness here on earth—as opposed to sacrificing his happiness now for rewards in "a better place" as preached by Christianity and Islam for example.

In ethics, her major contribution was in showing that acting in your self-interest is moral. Her view is based on a complete rejection of the concept of original sin and the view that man is inherently evil or depraved, constantly at war with his urges and instincts… always wanting to follow his lowly nature, but fighting hard to be "moral."

Her epistemology is based on reason as man's only means of knowledge. She defined reason as "the faculty that identifies and integrates the material provided by man's senses." It's the use of reason that elevates man to the conceptual level of thinking, in contrast to the perceptual level which we share with animals. Like Aristotle, she emphasized that reason employs a process of logic, which she defined as "the art of non-contradictory identification." She also pointed out that thinking is not automatic. She puts it this way in her essay on "Objectivist Ethics"...

Reason is a faculty that man has to exercise by choice. Thinking is not an automatic function. In any hour and issue of his life, man is free to think or to evade that effort.

Ayn Rand was aware that the American Revolution had been incomplete, *Atlas Shrugged*, and her philosophy of Objectivism, paves the way for completing the revolution by asserting the moral superiority of individual Liberty. As she stated in her essay, *"For the New Intellectual"*...

> The world crisis of today is a moral crisis – and nothing less than a moral revolution can resolve it: a moral revolution to sanction and complete the political achievement of the American Revolution.

She summarized the battle as the reason-egoism-capitalism axis vs. they mysticism-altruism-collectivism axis and I believe that is dead right.

While the Founders put the individual first and then attempted to design a system that would safeguard individual rights, the system ultimately failed because they tried to place their individualistic political philosophy on top of the anti-individualistic creed of Judeo-Christianity. That is a creed that emphasizes self-sacrifice and regards capitalism, money, and the profit motive as base, immoral, and even downright evil. Well, as the Bible says, when you troubleth your own house, you will inherit the wind.

The Revolution was also incomplete in the legal realm, as witnessed by the failure of the Constitution to stop the regulatory and welfare state of the 20th century, especially the New Deal. One can argue that it was not the Constitution that was at fault, but rather the failure of the courts to uphold the Constitution. That's true to a degree. However, even in the late 1800's, Constitutional law permitted both state and federal governments to regulate economic affairs that were reminiscent of the paternalistic English system, rather than consistent with the new system of individual liberty. This usually happened under the guise of "acting in the public interest," and preventing "monopolies" via Antitrust laws, such as the ones we discussed previously.

Constitutional protections of life, liberty and property have not been sufficient to protect us from the tyranny of the so-called "common good" or "public interest." We need to remember there is no such thing as the common good. The "public" is simply a collection of individuals. You cannot create any lasting good by violating the rights of the individual. You cannot create peace and prosperity through force and coercion. You cannot truly have freedom if your mind is shackled by religion, nor can you have it if your labor is shackled economically by socialism. In America, we must have freedom in both areas. We must have the liberty of hand and brain.

At bottom, the lesson of *Atlas Shrugged* is this: **the mind must be left free—force should be eradicated from all levels of human society if people are to flourish and grow**. Just as plants need sunlight and oxygen, we humans need reason and liberty.

Ayn Rand left a legacy of reason and freedom and a moral defense of capitalism that is desperately needed today if we are going to restore Liberty and complete the Revolution. I believe that her invaluable contributions to the cause of freedom will be remembered and revered far into the future, long after the books of the religionists and socialists have turned to dust.

With her exalted view of man, her reality-based metaphysics, her defense of individual rights and capitalism, and her focus on values and productive achievement as the way to happiness, Ayn Rand left a philosophy that is indeed worthy of America's founding ideals.

> Don't work for my happiness, my brothers — show me yours — show me that it is possible — show me your achievement — and the knowledge will give me courage for mine.
>
> – Ayn Rand, *The Fountainhead*

CHAPTER 12
THE ANIMATING CONTEST OF FREEDOM

To restore harmony... to render us again one people acting as one nation should be the object of every man really a patriot. The last hope of human liberty in this world rests on us.

If you are ever in Lexington, Massachusetts in April, there is a place where you can see ghosts. Guaranteed.

Every third Monday in April, at six in the morning, the ghosts appear on Lexington town green. Now, at first, they don't look like ghosts. At first they just look like a bunch of old guys dressed up in costumes, re-enacting the skirmish that started the American Revolution on April 19th, 1775.

You have to watch closely and pay attention to see the ghosts. First, you will see the Minutemen milling around on the green, with Captain Parker trying to organize them. You hear—and feel—the beating of the drums.

Before the locals are quite organized, the lines of redcoats appear, seemingly out of the morning mist, which is always a bit uncanny and eerie to behold because legend has it that's just how it happened on the actual day. Before the Minutemen knew it, the redcoats were on top of them, as if emerging from a fog.

But still, that's not when you see the ghosts. You and the rest of the crowd are still well aware that this is play acting. The British General Pitcairn begins to yell, "Lay down your arms you damn rebels, or you are all dead men!" You can see that the Minutemen are afraid, as well they should be, because there are only seventy of them facing a trained, professional army of more than two hundred, all with bayonets. There are shouts back and forth and the Minutemen begin to disperse and fall back... but before they can retreat a shot rings out… to this day, nobody knows from where.

Now the action begins, and now you will see the ghosts.

You will see the ghosts of the first Americans who had the courage to stand up for liberty. You will see their fear as the redcoats run at them, firing at point blank range, with flames leaping from their muskets. You will see the ghosts of the Redcoats overpowering the rebels amidst the fog of gunpowder and the steel flash of the bayonets. You will see eight of the rebels fall on the green and watch the rest run and retreat in the face of the onslaught. You will see the ghosts of the Redcoats stop the chase and then return slowly and calmly through the gunpowder fog to form the company. You will hear the drums again. And then, as quickly as they came, the ghosts are gone.

All of it takes only about four minutes. But in those four minutes, the ghosts have told you volumes. They have told you what Patrick Henry's phrase, "give me liberty or give me death," really means. They have told you about the price paid by all of the men and women that have worn the uniform of this country in battle. After you witness this battle, be careful you don't close your eyes when you get back home, because the lesson may lodge in your brain and cause you to see other ghosts…

You may see the ghosts of the brave men of Bunker Hill as they held off their onslaught. You may see Doctor Joseph Warren fall on that hill because he stood with the infantry even though he was an officer and not expected to fight... You may think of the starving, shoeless men in tatters during the winter at Valley Forge, who wrapped their feet in rags and stained the snow with their blood… You may see General Washington tearing into the fray at Trenton, giving no thought to his own safety, with musket balls whizzing over his head and hitting his horse…

You may remember the horrible clash of a Civil War and see oceans of ghosts dressed in blue and gray…. more than half a million before it was over…. You may remember the horrors of Gettysburg, Chickamauga, Chancellorsville and Shiloh…. and the terrible price paid to make the ideals of the Declaration of Independence a reality for all Americans.

You may think of the awful, bloody battles of World War I and all of the young American boys in foreign lands, caught up in a senseless European struggle we never should have entered… always remember that it was Americans who ended a fight we didn't start as one million of them bravely pushed through the Argonne to defeat the Germans while losing 117,000 in the process.

You may think of World War II and the oceans of crosses in France for those who fell on D-Day… of the 33, 000 men killed in the awful, long battle of the Hurtgen forest… Of the tens of thousands at Normandy… of Point Du Hoc and Omaha Beach… of the Battle of the Bulge… of those who endured the horrors of the Pacific campaigns… too many men and places to name, but in the end victorious.

Or you may think of all of those in Vietnam… of the men tortured at the "Hanoi Hilton"…. Of the hell they went through in the war and the hell that many of them were put through by un-grateful Americans when they got home. It was during that era when this country really started to turn into something different than what it had been…

And finally, you may think of all of the heroes of more recent times… who answered the call after September 11, 2001, and have suffered and fought, defended us and fallen in god-forsaken deserts in Iraq and remote mountains in Afghanistan…

… All of them heroes, all of them died defending Liberty. Some sleep on foreign shores and some sleep here in the land they made free and have been trying to keep free. For us.

How are we going to honor our courageous dead? Did they fight and die, only to have us betray our glorious revolution and turn this country over to the ideas of Karl Marx and Benito Mussolini?

Did they give their last measure of devotion for liberty, so we can betray them by acting like a nation of children, willing to give up our independence and liberty for the promise of suckling at the breast of a nanny state?

Did they endure the horrors of war and the separation from their families so we can become indentured servants to a rapacious government that consumes one-half of the national income, builds mountains of debt on the backs of our children and attacks those who work hard and prosper for wanting to keep the fruits of their own labor?

All Americans… ALL Americans… should answer these questions with a resounding NO!

To be an American is to hold Liberty as your highest value. It's to defend that "precious jewel" for yourself and fully respect the liberty of your fellow Americans.

Instead of betraying them, let us honor our heroes and secure a brighter future for our posterity.

How? By completing the Revolution.

We now need a second American Revolution, but not of arms, of ideas.

A Change In Hearts and Minds

Looking back on the American Revolution from 1818, John Adams commented that the real revolution occurred many years before 1776, the "real revolution," he said, was "in the hearts and minds of the people."

This is what we desperately need in America today… a complete paradigm shift so we wake up from our socialist stupor.

These are the times that try men's souls. The summer soldier and the sunshine patriot will,

> in this crisis, shrink from the service of their country; but he that stands it now, deserves the love and thanks of man and woman.
>
> – Thomas Paine, Common Sense, January 10, 1776

Many millions of Americans still believe in our founding principles, but feel frustrated. After all, what can we do? Despite our heritage, decade after decade, liberty has eroded and government has advanced. We are now at the end of the road and staring into the abyss.

Again, the Founders can offer us counsel:

> It does not require a majority to prevail, but rather an irate, tireless minority keen to set brushfires of freedom in the minds of men.
>
> — Samuel Adams, Father of the American Revolution

John Adams also pointed the way, when he said, "Let us presume, what is in fact true, that the spirit of Liberty is as ardent as ever among the body of the nation, though a few individuals may be corrupted." Unfortunately, that spirit if Liberty does not exist in America today. We have both hearts and minds to change. How can we do that? Here's how Adams did it…

> Let us tenderly and kindly cherish, therefore the means of knowledge. Let us dare to read, think, speak, and write. Let every order and degree among people rouse their attention and animate their resolution. Let them all become attentive to the grounds and principles of government. Let us read and recollect and impress upon our souls the views and ends of our own more immediate forefathers, in exchanging their native country for a dreary, inhospitable wilderness. Let us examine into the nature of that power, and the cruelty of that oppression, which drove them from their homes. Recollect their amazing fortitude, their bitter sufferings, — the hunger, the nakedness, the cold, which they patiently endured, — the severe labors of clearing their grounds, building their houses, raising their provisions, amidst dangers from wild beasts and savage men, before they had time or money or materials for commerce. Recollect the civil and religious principles and hopes and expectations which constantly supported and carried them through all hardships with patience and resignation. Let us recollect it was liberty, the hope of liberty for themselves and us and ours, which conquered all discouragements, dangers, and trials. — John Adams

The hope of Liberty. Not the false "hope" of handouts and unearned benefits that is peddled these days. Not the false hope that government will solve our problems. It was the hope of Liberty. That's the only enduring hope. That's the hope that animates the just and the good. It is the Spirit of Liberty that has to be restored and it can only be done through knowledge and education. We need to also remember that hope is not enough—we also have to fight for our Liberty.

Ronald Reagan was right when he said "freedom is never more than one generation away from extinction. We didn't pass it to our children in the bloodstream. It must be fought for, protected, and handed on for them to do the same, or one day we will spend our sunset years telling our children what it was once like in the United States when men were free."

Right now, the last remnants of freedom in America are less than a generation away from extinction.

Completing The Revolution

It is at the root where we have been attacked and it is at the root where we must strike back—by upholding the principle of Liberty consistently and intransigently.

I believe most people can be cured of this dreadful religio-socialist virus that has infected so many. They can be cured through education and by reaffirming America's original political philosophy and our commitment to Individual Rights. And we can complete the revolution by rejecting altruism and embracing a rational moral philosophy that holds individual liberty and happiness as its standard of value. The only thing that is required is the effort to study and think… plus a bit of intellectual courage.

It's critically important to think in terms of principles so we can apply the principles to concrete situations. It begins with a true understanding of Liberty and Individual Rights. That means we need to recognize the morality of the rights-based approach to political philosophy, and the immorality of the needs-based approach.

Once we understand that distinction, it is easy to see why the moral approach is also the one that produces the greatest results, or the "greatest happiness for the greatest number." This really should be no surprise, because why shouldn't the philosophy that is proper for an individual man also produce the best results for men in general?

We need to uphold the integrity of our own minds and never defer to others on "faith" or engage in "consensus thinking." Call every fact and opinion before "reason's tribunal," just as Jefferson counseled. If certain assertions and opinions of others don't pass the test, then we should reject them. That doesn't mean any individual is omniscient. We are all fallible and subject to error. Sometimes we have incomplete information, sometimes we have errors in our thinking; however, the only way to correct these errors is through reason.

With Individual Rights as our compass, a firm understanding of the morality of liberty, and a commitment to reason and critical thinking, we can then analyze politicians and policies using the compass of Individual Rights along with the map of a government limited for Liberty.

When looking at any proposed policy, first ask "is there any force or fraud involved here." If the answer is no, then it is none of the Government's business.

If the government is already involved, we can ask, "is Government acting within its proper scope as a "policeman" or protector of rights?" Or are they violating individual rights (it doesn't matter if the intention is a "good one") and engaging in legalized plunder. If the latter is the case, then we should oppose that policy.

When we hear about the wonderful free giveaways politicians are going to shower on various groups, we should always ask "at whose expense?" Remember that Government is not a productive entity. Every dime it has was taken from the pockets of citizens. That money is supposed to be used only to protect our individual rights to life, liberty, and property. When one group is promised some unearned benefit, then you know immediately it will be at the expense of another group. Government is then operating not as a protector, but as a violator of rights.

Above all, we should never apologize or feel guilty about being successful. We should take pride when we work hard to achieve our values, reach our goals, and live with integrity. We should have no problem telling politicians to keep their hands out of our pockets and that we will decide how to dispose of our own income.

We should also see modern politicians for what they are. We need to understand they have become corrupted and (with very few exceptions) are no longer "wise and noble statesmen" working to protect and defend our Constitution and Individual Rights. Let us stop being so naïve and giving them the benefit of the doubt for their "good intentions." The fact of the matter is, the relationship of a statist government to its citizens is similar to the relationship between a vampire and a human neck. This government is draining the lifeblood out of our country and we have nobody but ourselves to blame, because we keep putting these big government politicians into office. We need to start demanding they take the fangs out.

Above all, we need to also understand the purpose of a government in a free society is not to provide for the "needs" of the people—it is simply to protect their rights and legally uphold the moral principle that this country was founded on. This means a proper government does not do most of the things our government is now doing.

It does not manipulate interest rates… or force banks to lower lending standards… or steal money from taxpayers to bail out corporations… or steal money from taxpayers to pay for other people's health insurance… or steal money from "the rich" to give to "the poor"… or steal money from the poor and middle class to give to the rich… or take money from the young to give to the old… or tell businesses how they should run their operations… or prohibit freedom of speech prior to elections…. or tell doctors how much they can charge for their services…. or force employers or religious institutions to provide free birth control… or seize taxpayer money to subsidize "green" energy companies… or ban free men for drilling for oil on their own property or using coal to heat their homes… or give taxpayer money to community agitators like ACORN… or dictate what kind of programming private media outlets should offer… or send taxpayer money to foreign countries…. or takeover automobile companies and banks… or tell us how many gallons of water can go in a toilet or what type of light bulbs we can use… or fire CEO's in private industry… or ban smoking in private establishments…. or force people that are paying their own mortgages to pay the mortgages of their neighbors as well, etc, etc.

ALL of it is wrong. All of it is immoral and unconstitutional. And when you consider the fact that we are now $15 trillion in debt, with another $50 - $100 trillion in unfunded liabilities, all of it is madness!

What we should be doing is rebelling against this resurgence of big government and demanding it be rolled back to its proper size and put in its proper place. We should be fighting to put this monster back in its cage. We have to stop playing around the edges and realize the problem has become systemic and we need to change the system.

We need to start demanding a free society. A free society is one in which the government does not interfere in thought, production or trade. A free society is one in which the government is limited to one role: protecting the individual's right to his or her own life, liberty and property.

At the highest level, we need to take the Founder's principle of the Separation of Church and State and start advocating for the following as well:

1. A separation of Church and State.
2. A separation of Economics and State.
3. A separation of Science and State.
4. A separation of Education and State.

Why? For the same reason that the Founders separated Church and State: every individual has a right to believe whatever they want; however, they should not be allowed to impose their beliefs on others. You can believe in gods, ghosts, goblins, witches and the tooth fairy if you want… and you can further believe that they somehow tell you how to live your life… but because of the separation of Church and State you cannot impose those beliefs and dictates on others.

Perhaps your religious beliefs are crazy and irrational—or perhaps you are right and I am crazy and irrational and no doubt headed straight for hell—but it doesn't matter to society at large because neither of us can force our beliefs on one another since the government may not legally enforce one American's religious beliefs on any other American (at least for now).

It should be the same in all other areas of life. Perhaps you think that it's a great idea for the government to take money from taxpayers and give it to General Motors. If we had a separation of Economics and State, your opinion would go no further than that; because the government could not enforce that opinion on other Americans at the point of a gun. You would have to resort to going door-to-door and taking up a collection for General Motors. Good luck with that.

Or perhaps you decide to start a business and you become very successful. I see your success and your wealth and I decide that you have "too much" and you need to give a higher percentage of your income to the wonderful bureaucrats in our government so they can put it to better use, like giving it to "the poor." In a free society, my opinion would end there and if I wanted your money redistributed to the poor I would have to resort to robbing you at the point of a gun and then I'd have to go out and find some poor people to give it to. Liberals would never do that of course, because, although they want to feel morally superior, guns are scary, they don't venture into poor neighborhoods, and that scenario would be far too much work.

The same with Science. Let's pretend I am a devout follower of the Church of the Warming Globe and you own a stinky smelly coal factory that provides energy to heat people's homes. I've watched Al Gore's scary movie and I firmly believe that your production of C02 is somehow contributing to warming the entire planet to levels that will become dangerous to human life and therefore your emissions should be severely restricted or else you should be fined or shut down. In a free society, with a Separation of Science and State, my "scientific" opinion would remain nothing but hot air and I would pose no threat to your business.

As for Education in a free society, the government would get completely out of that business. Schools would all be private and have to compete on a level playing field. Bad teachers could no longer hide behind government unions. People that do not have children would not be forced to subsidize schools. The next generation of children would not be indoctrinated from an early age that our benevolent government is the solution to every problem and greedy, materialistic businessmen are the cause of most of our woes. Parents would have choices and excellence in education would become the norm through profit-making and competition.

A Second Renaissance or a New Dark Ages?

If more Americans (no matter what their party affiliation) were to understand the truth about all we have been discussing, and finally see how far we have come from our Founding principles… to understand that we are following the ideas, not of Jefferson, Adams and Madison, but of Marx, Mussolini and Stalin… to see that we are fighting against our own glorious Revolution that freed mankind from the tyranny of both Church and State… and to realize that we are going down a road that has ruined every other country that has traveled it… then I think we could finally unite again under the banner of Liberty and eventually turn the 21st century into a Second Renaissance.

It does not matter how long you have been infected with the religio-socialist virus—it's never too late to get rid of it. When you suddenly discover the drink you've been sipping contains poison, there is only one thing to do: throw away that drink!

The problem we are facing today is not only within America. As our own socialists strike at the root from the inside, we have militant Islamic terrorists (a throwback to the Dark Ages) and socialist-communist forces attacking from the outside. Remember, collectivists see individuals as mere cells in a larger organism. Since a country, or a nation, is nothing more than a collection of individuals, this mindset sees America as a cell in the larger organism of "global humanity."

Just as socialists in American seek to "redistribute" from the most productive to the less productive individuals, global socialists seek to redistribute from the most productive to the less productive countries. Organizations like the U.N., for example, are nothing more than transmission belts for socialism (and now Jihad). America—as the number one producer in the world—is to be sacrificed on the altar of the "needs of the global community."

Just as a rich man has no obligation to a poor man, a rich country has no obligation to a poor country. America, by virtue of its being the first country in history founded in freedom, its immense production, its scientific breakthroughs, its saving the free world in two World Wars and the Cold War, and its extreme generosity in foreign aid (both in men and money), does not owe anybody anything. In fact, we could pull back all our troops and stop all foreign aid this instant, and our balance sheet would be on the plus side for thousands of years in terms of what we've done for the "global community."

Since we are in the midst of a larger battle on a global scale, it is even more important that we have moral certainty that we are right in defending liberty and freedom. If we lose that sense of certainty about what we stand for and that it is good and right, then we are doomed.

As a case in point, consider the Britain of World War II vs. the Britain if today. In 1940, the people of Britain courageously stood their ground and fought on even though they came within an inch of losing the Battle of Britain. The German Luftwaffe engaged in an intensive bombing campaign which included "terror bombing" tactics on the civilian population. In September of 1940, Hitler decided to engage in a civilian bombing campaign which included massive attacks on major cities, including London. Hitler decided to make the bombing raids at night to increase the 'fear factor' and also to make people weaker by not allowing them to sleep properly. People in London slept in underground stations for protection. Prime Minister Winston Churchill remained in London during the Blitz and regularly visited areas destroyed by the Luftwaffe. To the people of London, he was one of them. Churchill could have easily removed himself from the dangers of German bombers of course, but he refused to. He stayed in a bombed out London along with those who suffered.

In a broadcast about the Blitz, coincidentally given on September the 11th, 1940, he said this:

> These cruel, wanton, indiscriminate bombings of London are, of course, a part of Hitler's invasion plans. He hopes, by killing large numbers of civilians, and women and children, that he will terrorize and cow the people of this mighty imperial city, and make them a burden and anxiety to the Government...Little does he know the spirit of the British nation, or the tough fibre of the Londoners...who have been bred to value freedom far above their lives. This wicked man, the repository and embodiment of many forms of soul-destroying hatred, this monstrous product of former wrongs and shame, has now resolved to try to break our famous Island race by a process of indiscriminate slaughter and

> destruction. What he has done is to kindle a fire in British hearts, here and all over the world, which will glow long after all traces of the conflagration he has caused in London have been removed.

The people of Britain survived and hung on during what may have been the most critical year in Western Civilization and eventually emerged victorious. Why? Because they were certain about who they were and what they stood for. As Churchill said, they valued their freedom more than their lives.

But when that certainty is lost, things fall apart quickly. Flash forward to the UK of 2011—a failing welfare state where the government controls upwards of 75% of the economy. The Britain of today is closer to the Anthony Burgess novel, A Clockwork Orange, than it is to the old Empire making its last stand in 1940. As Mark Steyn writes in his book After America:

> When a broke British government attempted to increase the cost of university education, students rampaged through Parliament Square, set fire to the statue of Lord Palmerston and urinated on that of Winston Churchill. This signature photograph of the riot showed a "student" swinging from the Union Flag on the Cenotaph the memorial to Britain's 700,000 dead from the Great War.

Steyn calls today's Britain, an "economically emaciated, strike-bound slough of despond" where the government runs pretty much everything. While Hitler and the Germans could not destroy the British Empire with their bombs, they eventually succeeded in bringing it down with something more powerful: their ideas. Hitler wasn't able to get to them, but Kant and Hegel did.

The French Enlightenment philosopher Montesquieu said, "the last sigh of liberty will be heaved by an Englishman." Well, he was wrong about that, because the Brits heaved it long ago and the last vestiges of liberty are now held by their progeny: America. It is now up to us to remember our past and make sure there is never a last sigh of liberty.

"The Founders Survive"

Our Founders were truly a unique group of heroes and we can never know too much about them. It is a tragedy and a disgrace that American schoolchildren are barely taught about them.

One of the most amazing stories is the saga of George Washington. If there is any Founder that deserves to be held up as godlike it is he. He was truly the "indispensable man" and I firmly do not believe this country would exist without that one individual.

Washington single-handedly created the Continental Army and somehow managed to hold it together for the eight long years it took to win that war. Unlike most of the other Founders, he put himself on the line physically time and time again. Over the course of the war, he had musket balls knock off his hat, tear his cape, rip through his clothes and kill his horses, but he was somehow never touched. Above all, the story of Washington is the story of fortitude, courage, perseverance, and an unyielding commitment to right and reason.

Although he had tremendous character and intelligence, he also had many flaws as all humans do. He could be hot-tempered at times and used poor judgment in several campaigns. In fact, after he had an initial success in driving the British out of Boston, his army suffered defeat after defeat. He failed to defend New York and had to retreat to Pennsylvania. With that, much of the army disbanded and large numbers of civilians (including Washington's own mother) went over the British and became loyalists.

By December of 1776 his rag-tag army was in shambles. That's when he had a bold idea that he would implement on Christmas night. He started by reading the troops some words that came from the lantern-lit quill of a private in the Army. The Private's name was Thomas Paine:

> By perseverance and fortitude we have the prospect of a glorious issue; by cowardice and submission, a sad choice of a variety of evils—a ravaged country—a depopulated city—habitations without safety, and slavery without hope…

He hoped that the words would help them keep their courage a little longer. That night he planned to take a thousand men, along with horses and cannons, across the Delaware and march to Trenton, which was nine miles away, for a surprise attack on the British troops stationed there.

It was an incredible gamble, and the snow and sleet that night made matters worse. But Washington was determined. They made the perilous crossing after midnight and then Washington himself led them into Trenton where they did take the British and Hessians by surprise. It was such a surprise, the Americans lost no men that day and suffered only four wounded while capturing 800 prisoners. With this victory, morale improved and more recruits joined the Continental army.

However, this was the way it went for the rest of the struggle—many defeats with small victories here and there. By the next winter, things had turned very bleak again when the British took Philadelphia and popular support once again eroded. The army retreated to Valley Forge where conditions were every bit as bad as the history books say. While the troops were there, Congress declared a "Continental Thanksgiving" for them which included a special dinner. It consisted of "half a gill of rice and a tablespoon of vinegar."

At the center, it was always Washington holding things together and persevering. Somehow, he kept his army together until Cornwallis made his fatal blunder at Yorktown, by camping with his back to the sea and without naval cover. With the help of French forces, Yorktown was attacked from both land and sea and Cornwallis was forced to surrender. Suddenly the war was over and Washington had succeeded against all odds. However, this triumph was short-lived for Washington as it was marred by personal tragedy when his stepson Jacky died of camp fever, which he caught while serving as an aide to Washington in the Yorktown campaign.

Soon after the end of the War, Washington voluntarily gave up power by bidding his officers farewell at Fraunces Tavern in New York and resigning as commander of the armies. Aristocratic Europe was stunned by this and King George III called him the "greatest character of the age" because of this act.

Washington had earned the admiration and respect of the entire country and became the one person the people trusted above anyone else. In 1783, after the war had ended, there was a lot of dissatisfaction in the ranks of the Continental Army because most of the soldiers had not been paid for years. They were still being held up and delayed in waiting for their pay before they could be disbanded. The grumbling reached a climax when several of the officers planned and held a secret meeting to seek "justice." In other words, they were going to discuss a military coup.

To the great surprise of the mutinous officers, when they started the meeting, in walked Washington. He had written a short speech. As he took it out of his coat pocket, he said, "Gentlemen, you will permit me to put on my spectacles, for I have not only grown gray, but almost blind in the service of my country." He went on to shame them for even thinking about betraying the revolution and brought many of them to tears. Mutiny over.

If only General Washington were here now to shame the mass of our countrymen for betraying the revolution as well.

Another truly amazing story, is the unique relationship—and the deaths—of Adams and Jefferson. In their later years, they had settled old political differences and become great friends, keeping up an ongoing correspondence for many years. They both lived to ripe old ages.

Yes, as a matter of fact, it was the fourth. It was the 4th of July, 1826—Adams and Jefferson both died on the 4th of July, 50 years to the day from the signing of the Declaration of Independence. Think about that.

A few days before, the 83-year old Jefferson had written the following words in response to an invitation he received to an event celebrating the 50th anniversary of the signing of the Declaration. He replied that he was too frail to make the event, but sent this blessing regarding the Declaration of Independence and the significance of the July fourth anniversary:

> May it be to the world, what I believe it will be, (to some parts sooner, to others later, but finally to all) the signal of arousing men to burst the chains under which monkish ignorance and superstition had persuaded them to bind themselves, and to assume the blessings and security of self-government. That form which we have substituted, restores the free right to the unbounded exercise of reason and freedom of opinion. All eyes are opened, or opening, to the rights of man. The general spread of the light of science has already laid open to every view the palpable truth, that the mass of mankind has not been born with saddles on their backs, nor a favored few booted and spurred, ready to ride them legitimately, by the grace of God. These are grounds of hope for others. For ourselves, let the annual return of this day forever refresh our recollections of these rights, and an undiminished devotion to them...

It is true that even with the full knowledge and understanding of what Liberty really means, some men will still advocate the Old World philosophies of Authority, collectivism and forced sacrifice… or they will just not have the courage to take the medicine because of the responsibility freedom requires.

To them, what can be said? I can think of nothing better than what Samuel Adams said to the Americans of his generation who did not have the courage to fight for their Liberty and break the bonds of their own "tranquil" servitude…

> Contemplate the mangled bodies of your countrymen, and then say, What should be the reward of such sacrifices? Bid us and our posterity bow the knee, supplicate the friendship, and plow, and sow, and reap, to glut the avarice of the men who have let loose on us the dogs of war to riot in our blood and hunt us from the face of the earth? If ye love wealth better than liberty, the tranquility of servitude than the animating contest of freedom—go from us in peace. We ask not your counsels or arms. Crouch down and lick the hands which feed you. May your chains sit lightly upon you, and may posterity forget that ye

were our countrymen!

It's time for all Americans who love our lives and our liberty to stand up and be counted. Let's engage in the animating contest of freedom. Let's get off of our knees and throw away the security blankets of god-worship and state-worship. Let's stop acting like serfs, thankful for the crumbs thrown to us by politicians after they've stolen the entire loaf of bread.

In addition to truly understanding and honoring America's Founding Fathers, let's also heed these words of the great Ayn Rand…

> In the name of the best within you, do not sacrifice this world to those who are its worst. In the name of the values that keep you alive, do not let your vision of man be distorted by the ugly, the cowardly, the mindless in those who have never achieved his title. Do not lose your knowledge that man's proper estate is an upright posture, an intransigent mind and a step that travels unlimited roads. Do not let your fire go out, spark by irreplaceable spark, in the hopeless swamps of the approximate, the not-quite, the not-yet, the not-at-all. Do not let the hero in your soul perish, in lonely frustration for the life you deserved, but have never been able to reach. Check your road and the nature of your battle. The world you desired can be won, it exists, it is real, it is possible, it's yours.
>
> But to win it requires your total dedication and a total break with the world of your past, with the doctrine that man is a sacrificial animal who exists for the pleasure of others. Fight for the value of your person. Fight for the virtue of your pride. Fight for the essence of that which is man: for his sovereign rational mind. Fight with the radiant certainty and the absolute rectitude of knowing that yours is the Morality of Life and that yours is the battle for any achievement, any value, any grandeur, any goodness, any joy that has ever existed on this earth.

To honor our heroes and secure freedom for our children, every American needs to stand up and grab the torch of Liberty. Hold it high. And never let it go again.

Long Live Lady Liberty!

www.ingramcontent.com/pod-product-compliance
Lightning Source LLC
Chambersburg PA
CBHW020957160726
47994CB00006B/2262
* 9 7 9 8 5 4 4 5 1 8 9 7 6 *